I WAS A
STAGE DOOR
JOHNNY

by

John Hannam

Foreword by
BOB MONKHOUSE, OBE

I WAS A STAGE DOOR JOHNNY

by John Hannam

From an original idea by Mike Reader

COACH HOUSE PUBLICATIONS LIMITED

This book is dedicated to Dad

ISBN No. 1-899-392-149

© 1999 Coach House Publications Ltd

Published by Coach House Publications Ltd
The Coach House, School Green Road, Freshwater, Isle of Wight, PO40 9BB

Typeset by K·F·Typography
Ward Road, Totland Bay, Isle of Wight, PO39 0BD

Printed by The West Island Group
Afton Road, Freshwater, Isle of Wight, PO40 9TT

CONTENTS

FOREWORD BY BOB MONKHOUSE, OBE

There used to be a regular feature in *Reader's Digest* called 'The Most Unforgettable Character I Ever Met'. In any list of Unforgettable Characters I've Ever Met I'd certainly have to include the man who wrote this book, the irrepressible John Hannam.

John's an enthusiast and his passion is show business. He knows more about the stars than they do about themselves. Thankfully he's also discreet. He leaves the celebrities' dirty linen to their own private laundering.

That's not to say that you won't find among the following pages some fascinating tales about the famous folk he's met. That's because show people admire John's sedulous preparation for each interview and they tend to relax and open up to him. They tell John the sort of secrets that are kept from most journalists.

His reviews in our show biz weekly *The Stage* are highly regarded and notable for their total honesty. Luckily, performers who might take offence at criticism from other reviewers are generally appreciative of John's frankness. His opinions are constructive. He once wrote of me that I was much too sexy for comedy and I wasn't offended one tiny bit.

I know he has a great affection for comedians and I'm always aware when he's in the audience. His infectious laugh is sometimes a godsend for us onstage for it can get the audience going. During one of my Isle of Wight seasons he seemed to be there every night. It made me work that much harder to include new and topical material for each show so that he wouldn't be bored.

As you read this book you may come to the conclusion that its author is a bit of a softie. You'd be right. One of the reasons people like me come to trust John and respond warmly to him is the sweetness of his nature. While he loves a drop of wicked gossip to spice up his day, he is essentially a gentle and generous man. It's that endearing quality that makes his writing quite unique in the world of entertainment.

By the way, should you ever be short of a taxi service to run you around the charms of the Isle of Wight, I can personally recommend John. He's provided me with free transport so often that I've become used to the sound of my own terrified screams. When I say that he's driven me to a nervous breakdown I'm being literal. In short, he drives like he talks – nonstop.

I still think the title of this work shouldn't really be in the past tense. Oh yes, I know these are memoirs and such a happy recollection of his days and nights as a Stage Door Johnny. But he still is and always will be that same starstruck fan of greasepaint and spotlights and costumes and bravado. A Stage Door Johnny for life.

Enjoy John's first book – it's written from the heart.

CHAPTER ONE

TIN BATH, WIRELESS & STAGE DOORS

FORTY YEARS ago the idea of writing a book following over two thousand interviews with famous people would not even have been a remote dream. I was shy, blushed profusely and could not even cope with dining out in restaurants. There were times when I almost couldn't face the world around me and was close to tears at my self-inflicted hell.

I've never forgotten that struggle of self-confidence. Now when I look back at interviews with Sir Cliff Richard, Prince Edward and Terry Waite, I wonder just what I was even doing there. Is it all an act? Am I portraying John Hannam, interviewer?

How could I address 15,000 in a football stadium or entertain 300 guests at a sports dinner? Perhaps it's best if I don't think about it.

A stage door Johnny at age ten. The freckles and smile are still there but something else has long departed.

When I was growing up on the Isle of Wight, in Old Road, East Cowes, radio was the only mass entertainment media. My earliest heroes were Ted Ray, Peter Brough and Archie Andrews, Dick Barton, that pre-Bond special agent, and Doc, Lemmy, Jet and Mitch from *Journey Into Space*. Sunday lunchtimes were just made for *Family Favourites* and then Billy Cotton.

Friday nights were always something a little special, too. A tin bath in front of a real fire, *Ray's A Laugh* on the radio and dad arriving home late from the *County Press*, with his free copy of the next day's paper.

My late father, Roy, was a home movie enthusiast and there are still numerous films around of me from just six months old – in black and white, of course. He was also a great cinema movie fan with his very own 16 mm sound projector at home. We saw so many films.

A family friend, Den Watson, who worked at Osborne House, was the projectionist for the convalescent home that occupied much of Queen Victoria's favourite residence. Their weekly movies always arrived the night before they were due to be shown to the officers. Den would cover them over in his old van and sneak them out to our house. The official explanation would have been that they were being tested for the following night's Osborne House screening. On occasions I joined Den and dad in the projection room and even put on the interval records.

When dad was off work, following a heart attack, part of his recovery period was spent watching movies at the Royalty, Cowes, or the Kings at East Cowes. In the school holidays I was an eager companion. I can still remember watching Bonar Colleano and Dirk Bogarde in *Once A Jolly Swagman*, a speedway story. Many years later I interviewed another of the film's stars, Bill Owen of *Last of the Summer Wine* fame.

My mother, Ena, and dad, both former racing cyclists with the Vectis Roads Cycling Club, were great fans of the big band era and made regular visits to Sandown and Shanklin to see the hit bands of the time. Dad's great hero was Nat Gonella. Sadly, he died before I got to interview Britain's greatest-ever trumpet star.

Mum and Dad – fifty-seven happy years, on and off their bikes.

In the early '50s few parents could afford proper holidays. We had days out instead. The highlights for me were the visits to Portsmouth to watch variety and summer shows. Would we strike lucky and catch a huge star at the Theatre Royal? Imagine my disappointment, on one occasion, to discover Laurel and Hardy were live at the Royal the very next week. Not even the trolley bus ride could console me.

My first singing idol – Tony Brent. Picture given at stage door.

Before our very first visit I bought a lined red notebook to collect autographs – and still have it. The excitement for me was waiting at the stage door for the artistes to arrive. Meeting my first-ever singing idol, Tony Brent, was a memory that's never left me. His signed photo still looks as good as new. Others we saw at the Theatre Royal, now reopened in the '90s, were Michael Bentine, the Skyliners, a brilliant singing act, Brian Reece, radio's PC49, and a very young Harry Secombe.

There was one person, a young comedian at the very bottom of the bill, who actually refused to sign my book. I never forgot his name and he went on to become quite famous. Over thirty years later I was offered the chance to interview that very same person, at Padmore House, Whippingham. He was so charming.

2

We undertook a perfect interview session for the *Isle of Wight Weekly Post* and enjoyed a social chat and drink at the end. Dare I dig up the memory of that earlier refusal? He took it so well and even had the reason why.

He had begun writing all his own material, most successfully. During that week at Portsmouth, on the Monday band-call the manager told him another comic had done the same routine a few weeks earlier. His very own script had been pirated by a far less innovative comedian. For that reason, he was, quite rightly, grumpy all that week. Barry Took willingly signed on this occasion.

Up the road from the Theatre Royal was the Empire, now a supermarket. This was a number two or three theatre, which meant the quality of shows was not as good. Latterly, tatty nude shows were their stock in trade. From a city full of sailors there was a ready and waiting audience. We did go to some of the variety shows in 1950 and once saw Frankie Vaughan in only his third week as a professional entertainer.

At nearby Southsea, on the South Parade Pier, the resident summer season shows were something special. You could enjoy afternoon tea to the sounds of the top radio organists like Reginald Porter-Brown and then watch the first house of the Arthur English and 'Monsieur' Eddie Gray end-of-the-pier show. Arthur, the original spiv comedian, wore huge ties and had the famous catch phrase "Open the cage". He went on to become a very successful actor in television series like *Are You Being Served?* and *In Sickness and In Health*.

I'd never forgotten the impact Arthur English had on me. It was stars like him who created my love for front cloth comedians. On two occasions, back in the '80s, I tried to interview Arthur. He was due to come to Ryde to open a shop in Union Street. Sadly he was ill and could not attend. A year or two later I made arrangements to visit him at his home in Aldershot. Before we ever got to meet he was rushed into hospital. I did have a quick chat when I later 'phoned the hospital but he never really recovered from that illness.

Visits to the Portsmouth theatres, particularly the Royal, where the numbers flashed up as the new acts came on stage, made a lasting impression on me. My love for showbiz people and live shows came from those day outings. Despite television, radio, movies, video, music and books, live theatre is still my greatest passion. As a schoolboy I wrote to many stars for autographs and photos. I always seemed to get replies, from names like Wilfred Pickles, Jon Pertwee, Billy Daniels, Dave King and Connie Francis.

Back on the Isle of Wight it was not quite so easy to see the stars, who, when here, were mainly in Sandown and Shanklin. The once-nightly shows meant it was virtually impossible for me to travel back home across the Island late at night.

The Ryde Commodore had occasional live shows which were always easier to attend. In the late '50s and early '60s when stars like Dusty Springfield and Matt Monro, both sadly taken from us much too early, came to Ryde, transport was such a lot simpler. There were also top pop groups like the Animals and solo stars including Marty Wilde and Lonnie Donegan.

CHAPTER TWO

BUMP IN THE NIGHT

THE SUNDAY concerts at Sandown Pavilion and Shanklin Theatre were memorable occasions. Fountain Garage later ran coaches from Cowes and the stars performed two shows within three hours. They closed the first half at Shanklin, the smaller venue, and then took a taxi ride to top the bill at Sandown.

The late Don Moody, the local council's entertainments manager, attracted all the real top names of the time. There was Petula Clark, Dickie Valentine, Gary Miller, Dick Emery, Terry Scott and Hugh Lloyd, Eve Boswell, Tommy Trinder and a young upstart comic named Jimmy Tarbuck. What an autograph hunter's dream!

One milestone from growing up in East Cowes was watching the maiden flight of the Saunders-Roe Princess flying boat on August 22, 1952. What a day that was! Geoff Tyson, the pilot, was an instant local hero. I never failed to be excited by seeing the flying boat in the air.

Once, in the Solent, I saw the Saunders-Roe aircraft known as the "Squirt", the SR A1 tiny jet flying boat, hit a piece of driftwood and sink. Also, viewing the passenger liners from Castle Point, as they passed to

I've never forgotten seeing the maiden flight of the Princess flying boat.

and from Southampton, made a welcome change from chasing the local girls.

A not so happy memory of life as a fourteen-year-old schoolboy was one of my sleep walking escapades. In the middle of the night, around 2 a.m., I climbed out of my upstairs bedroom window and dropped fifteen feet below into the flower bed, waking up as I flattened the tulips.

Imagine my parents' reaction when they heard me calling from the front garden. After that, my window was blocked up and would only open about six inches. It made my other exploits, like getting a pea stuck up my nose and pouring a bucket of soot over my head (so that's why I've lost my hair), seem far less harrowing.

Sport has always been a great part of my life, particularly in the early days when people played for fun. There were obvious highlights, like becoming the Hampshire mile champion at fifteen and running in the All-England championships. At that time I was a pupil at Cowes Secondary School, which

Winning the Hampshire boys' mile championship at Southampton in 1957.

still brings back such happy memories. Teachers like Vic Reed, Bill Capps, John Price, Roy Templeton and 'Nanner' Weeks were legends in their own right.

A few years earlier when Grange Road, another marvellous school, had reached the Primary League play-off final, against deadly rivals Cowes Denmark Road, at Westwood Park, I was regrettably off school with German measles. Football master Bill Reed, a gem of a teacher and a real nice guy, was tearing his hair out. Then there was good news. Dr Fraser Down, who had initially suggested my name to mum and dad, said I could play. I was the East Cowes goalkeeper who got cheered off the field. It was some compensation for losing 2-0. My grandparents even had a wooden case made, with J.H. on the side, to carry my gear in.

A few months earlier I had not been cheered off the field. I know there were a few tears. A hundred yards from home, at the old Saunders-Roe sports ground, Grange Road had met Barton in a cup tie. Unbeaten in the league and with only one goal conceded, we were thrashed 6-0 by our brilliant opponents. The 'Boneheads' had struck again. They had so many talented youngsters like Brian Greening, Keith Mitchell, Monty Burton and a young winger called Terry Perkins, who banged three goals past me. A few years later he was to change the course of my life.

One of my greatest motivations is to see Islanders succeed, in whatever field. I can remember seeing J. B. Priestley on a Cowes to Southampton paddle steamer. At that time he lived at Brook. Cliff Michelmore was born in Cowes and went on to become such a famous television personality. Marion Lincoln, from Newport, was nearly as famous as her comedian husband, Nat Jackley. Nettlestone's Roy Shiner also banged in so many goals for Sheffield Wednesday. Another local youngster, Les Maskell, went on to play for Norwich City. The Yarmouth-based Smith brothers had sailed the Atlantic in their tiny boat. Uffa Fox was a world-famous helmsman and boat designer. Their successes filled me with such pride. Later I'll reveal how I tracked down several other famous Islanders for personal interviews.

I was so excited when a young Newport milkman was signed by Decca

Records, after winning a local talent contest at Newport's Medina Cinema. Top London agent Bunny Lewis changed his name to Craig Douglas. All of a sudden he was on *Six-Five Special*.

I had enjoyed pop music since discovering those early '50s crooners, like Tony Brent, Dickie Valentine, Ronnie Hilton and Gary Miller. At that time my father had a 'tape pal' in Lexington, Tennessee – they exchanged message tapes instead of letters. Then in the midst of British hits like *How Much Is That Doggie In The Window?* came special tapes of a new American singer, who was completely unknown in Britain.

His records hadn't even been released over here. I had an American tape with them all on. It was, of course, Elvis Presley. I became an instant fan. Going to church on a Sunday night was always so enjoyable at Adelaide Grove, particularly when I was going home to play my Elvis tape. He became world famous and then in his wake came some of my other personal favourites like Buddy Holly, Duane Eddy, Rick Nelson and the Everly Brothers.

Suddenly, in 1959, young Craig Douglas was outselling some of them in the pop charts, or hit-parade as it was then. With my father working as a linotype operator at the *Isle of Wight County Press*, I used to write all the latest news of Craig Douglas for the paper and even got the odd by-line. Over many years I wrote numerous Craig stories for the *County Press*.

I finally met Craig, this time without his football boots on, outside Ryde's Commodore Cinema, back in the summer of '59. We became friends and have remained so ever since.

Following his career, via visits to Weston-Super-Mare, Southend, Scotland, Bournemouth and London, broadened my outlook and I had the chance to meet other famous people.

What a lovely couple! Craig and Heather.

Gradually, my shyness disappeared. By this time I'd met my wife, Heather, in Newport's Ideal Snack Bar, then in Pyle Street. We just happened to lunch there every day. I was working for Gould, Hibberd and Randall, the gold medal soft drinks firm located in Church Litten, where Marks and Spencer now stands.

I eventually plucked up courage to ask her out. That took some doing – and I blushed even more when she said yes. Her support and confidence was a great morale booster – and still is. At times my unsociable working hours have, quite understandably, proved difficult for her to contend with. I thank Heather for her tolerance. On the bonus side, she has met so many of her favourite stars and some remain friends, like Russ Conway and Frankie Vaughan.

In 1972 I visited the Isle of Wight Hospital Radio studios at St Mary's, to talk sport with local *Echo* journalist Maurice Leppard. At that time I was the founding secretary of the Isle of Wight Southampton FC Supporters' Club. Many will remember him for his Stumper cricket column in the *County Press*, back in the '50s. Maurice is such a gentleman and, dare I say it, too nice to be a hard-bitten news journalist. He's also very persuasive, too. The following week I was asked back to join Hospital Radio's sports team.

My confidence blossomed with more hospital radio exposure and, eventually, I was asked to join their *Late Date* presenters. This has always been their most popular programme. It's the nightly request show. Before the programme, the idea was to visit the wards to obtain requests. Some of the requests, particularly from the ladies' ward, didn't always involve records – and a few of the nurses were just as cheeky.

On my *Late Date* shows I featured the odd interview recorded on an old cassette recorder, the first being the Bachelors, which was set up by Craig Douglas. They sussed this shy red-faced Islander was as naïve as they come and gave me a rough ride. Mind you, at that time, their egos made them more than a little arrogant.

I suffered my way through that début interview. Many years later, when they were ageing and fading pop stars, I was able to give them as good as they gave me in a return contest. Now there are two Bachelors groups on the road, one containing Con and Dec Cluskey and the other fronted by John Stokes. Perhaps it's justice.

Then came a brand new hospital radio series, *John Hannam Meets The Entertainers*.

Hospital radio is a great training ground for broadcasters. The local group, who have a well appointed St Mary's studio, initially served four local hospitals. In their formative years people like Jill Swallow, Pat Norris, Peter Baxter, Ian Thrippleton, John Primmer, Mike Cooley, Rosemary Shackleton, Frank Jellis, Steve Knapp, Dennis Chubb, Mildred Morris and Dave Holbrook did much to get them off the ground. Now others are following suit.

In more recent years several Isle of Wight Hospital Radio presenters have gone on to become top professional broadcasters with prestigious mainland and national stations. Those that spring to mind include Richard Pocock, who changed his name to Rick Jackson for Power FM, James Hemming who went on to commercial stations in Oxford and London, Andy Shier, a founder member of Isle of Wight Radio, and Duncan Kennedy, now at BBC Television News. For me, hospital radio was the thrill of broadcasting to an audience. We'd all played around on home tape recorders but this was like the real thing and you were giving a service to people who needed cheering up. It can be very satisfying. One letter I had from a nun, who had a spell in St Mary's, made it all worth while.

Having written to so many famous people during my school days for autographs and pictures, it was a dream to visit theatres, hotels and clubs to record interviews for *John Hannam Meets The Entertainers*. With the skill of my talented producer Dave Holbrook, many of the interviews were made into a series of early chat shows. Apparently, some are still occasionally played on the station more than twenty-five years later. I hope I've got better since then. Now I wince when I hear them.

I quickly learnt that to be in awe of the stars I interviewed just didn't work. Being confronted with faces you knew from television series or record covers was certainly daunting. To appear nervous, inhibited by their presence or clearly embarrassed by being in such esteemed company, was detrimental to getting the best out of your guests.

Hence, very early on, I decided to try and assume a different personality. Somehow I needed to project an air of confidence and assurance that enabled me to set up an instant rapport with my interviewee. Most of those early interviews were only ten minutes – so my reactions had to be virtually instant. I love showbusiness people anyway and have always given them the respect they deserve. A please and thank you can mean so much.

CHAPTER THREE

DOING MY HOMEWORK

Homework is the principal key to any successful interview. I've seen and heard numerous interviewers who have no idea about their guests. Many merely bluff their way through and it clearly shows. Sadly, at both local and national level, too many presenters just seem to want to top their guests, whoever they are. It's all about self-inflated egos. They believe their own publicity. That's a fatal mistake. In any form of chat or talk show the guests should be the stars.

From my initial days as an interviewer, doing the preparation has always been as equally rewarding as the actual interview. There is such a fascination discovering little known facts about famous people. I'll spend hours reading books. Back in the '70s I went to a Sandown hotel to interview '60s pop star Ricky Valance, at an Isle of Wight Rock 'n' Roll Society gig. Ricky's only hit had been *Tell Laura I Love Her*. My request for a chat wasn't warmly received. He, quite obviously, was not too bothered.

"I'll do it but if you ask stupid or uninteresting questions, I'll just pack up and walk away,"threatened Ricky. Not the attitude I was looking for, although I had by now relished the challenge. After a couple of warm-up questions I asked him about the days he was a male model in Wales. Suddenly his whole perception changed. "How the hell did you know that?" were his exact words. There was no problem after that. I'd gleaned that information from an old paperback on '60s music.

Now Ricky and I have become good friends. When he came to Sandown Pavilion, back in the summer of '96, his whole attitude to life had changed, as he'd recently discovered Christianity. He also readily admitted he once had an ego problem and had been a pain in the ass to so many people. One-hit wonders often have that tendency.

With regard to Ricky's career, he was so unlucky. That number one was so hard to follow. I didn't know, until quite recently, that Norrie Paramor first offered that song to Craig Douglas but he turned it down. The death dirge wasn't really suited to his image. Rick's version was brilliant and still sounds good. He made many other great singles and deserved much more chart success.

The release of Diamond Records' CD of all his old singles proves that. He once toured with Island '60s singer Pat Reader and I had the privilege of reintroducing them to each other during a '70s gig at the Ponda Rosa. Pat even had Joe Meek produce a couple of her singles. Now she's a local nurse and as bubbly as ever. I had a crush on her at school and can still see why.

When I went to the Metropole Hotel, on Ventnor seafront, to meet South African singer Eve Boswell for my hospital radio show, I just couldn't keep my eyes off her. She looked wonderful and, on her own admission, was searching for another husband. Was it a hint? I very much doubt it. Sadly, she died in 1998. There was so much more to her than *Pickin' A Chicken*.

Meeting Felix Bowness, Fred Quilly from *Hi-de-Hi*, for the first time was an unforgettable experience. In the '60s and '70s he'd been a regular in the Sandown Pavilion summer season shows. I turned up at his Ventnor Winter Gardens give-away show to tape an interview. I spotted him in the 'phone box. We did twenty hilarious minutes, backstage, with so many ad libs. It was vintage Bowness. When I discovered the record button was not pushed in I felt physically sick. He took it well. The re-run was nowhere near as good.

Felix, one of life's perpetual worriers, is such a gifted comedian, as thousands of television warm-ups will testify. All the top stars insisted he performed their pre-show entertainment. Many years after that Ventnor meeting he caught me out at the London Palladium, no less.

My wife Heather and myself were celebrating our 25th wedding anniversary in October 1988. The late Wally Malston, an Islander who went on to write thousands of television scripts for shows like *Winner Takes All*, *The Golden Shot*, *3-2-1*, *Play Your Cards Right* and *The Generation Game*, invited us to spend the week-end at his Fleet home and travel up with him on the Sunday to *Live From The Palladium*. He was the chief scriptwriter.

I wasn't smiling when Felix Bowness caught me out in front of a Palladium full house.

This meant watching the rehearsals, meeting some of the stars like Marti Caine, Mark Walker and Sinitta, and enjoying all the in-house hospitality that goes with it. It was quite a day. We'd visited the exclusive private estate where Jimmy Tarbuck lived and had a London lunch with Craig Douglas at his Dolphin Square apartment, overlooking the Thames. Then he drove us to the Palladium for the afternoon run through.

During the tea interval we were spotted by Felix Bowness who, unbeknown to us, was there as the show's warm-up comedian. "There's that bleedin' John Hannam from the Isle of Wight" were the words that flew across the crowded hospitality suite. We'd been sat next to The Art Of Noise. As always, Felix was so pleased to see us. He hinted I might be hearing from him later in the night. If so, would I just say January 1st. That seemed painless.

The atmosphere became electric as the rehearsals ended and the capacity audience filed in. Can I now set the scene. The Palladium was bursting with a full house of 2,300. Tom Jones was topping the bill. The excitement was fever pitch with the orchestra tuning up. Then came the on-stage arrival of Felix Bowness, with barely 15 minutes left to the start of the live television broadcast. We were sat in the front row of the dress circle, with a perfect view. Unfortunately my friend, for want of a better word, Felix Bowness, could clearly see us. He got into his comedy routine and everyone was on a high and he was doing his job. Then came the words we didn't really want to hear.

"Sat up there in the front row are two friends of mine from the Isle of Wight, celebrating their 25th wedding anniversary. Stand up you two," bawled Felix. Heather was rooted to her seat, in fright, so it was left to me. Felix then went on to add that it was also my birthday. The full Palladium orchestra struck up the happy birthday tune with the audience joining in – and my long-forgotten blush suddenly made an encore. Then Felix added: "It is your birthday isn't it?" My reply of no, it's January 1st, brought the house down.

Highly embarrassed I sat down and remarked we were safe as no-one knew us in the audience. That was a rash statement. After the show a lady from Cowes, whose daughter worked with me at the *Weekly Post*, raced up to find us. What a small world.

There was a happy ending. During the end-of-show party, I was allowed to go on to the middle of the Palladium stage and look out on that vast, now empty, theatre. It was an exhilarating experience, particularly when I realised who had stood there in past years.

Once during a training course in Bristol I left the boring evening sessions in the bar to visit the Theatre Royal, Bath. It was far better than talking shop. My mission, other than to enjoy a show in this historic venue, was to seek an interview with Sylvia Syms. In our hastily improvised recording she revealed stories of one of my all time comedy giants, Tony Hancock.

They had worked on the movie *The Punch and Judy Man*. I still count myself so lucky to have seen two live Tony Hancock theatre appearances, both at the Kings, Southsea. He actually appeared twice at Sandown Pavilion and Shanklin Theatre, before his real fame, in Sunday concerts on June 22, 1952 and August 30, 1953.

One Christmas Eve on hospital radio we did a live link-up with a west country station. I had pre-recorded a spot with Roy Castle, one of the nicest and most genuine people I've ever met. A few minutes after it was played on air, the Bristol HBA station asked if Roy could chat with them. We had to quickly say he'd rushed off to get the last ferry home.

During my career I interviewed Roy on several occasions and it was always such an enjoyable experience. Following the first diagnosis of his cancer, Roy put up such a brave fight. There was a time when it looked as if he might have cracked it. He went back to work and was an inspiration to others.

The very last time I saw Roy was at a cancer charity night at the Kings, Southsea, when he was the star attraction. We met in a nearby hotel and he was on a real high, having been given a clean bill of health. What a night that was! Sadly, his good news was not to last. What a loss he was. Such a perfect man.

Roy Castle – a true gentleman. At Ryde's Ponda Rosa he met old friend Bob Muir (see Chapter Five).

So many youngsters worshipped him for *Record Breakers*. I still treasure his letters, signed with his own personal drawings.

Among other great personal memories of hospital radio interviews was one with the irrepressible Margaret Powell, whose books on life below stairs, in the days of servants, proved best sellers. I met her at an Isle of Wight Grocers' Association dinner at the Trouville Hotel, Sandown. She was such great company but with that infectious laugh it was hard to be serious. Meeting Colin Crompton, the cloth-capped chairman of the hit TV show the *Wheeltappers' and Shunters' Social Club*, and a former winner of the British *Song For Europe*, Bryan Johnson, were other happy occasions.

CHAPTER FOUR

A NEW DIRECTION

T HE OPPORTUNITY to write for a new monthly Island magazine, *The Wightman*, offered the chance of a new direction. The first edition went on sale in September, 1971 and I was given the task of writing a showbiz column and reviewing local shows. The experience proved invaluable and I got to meet all the right people. That was just about all I did get. When the magazine finally disappeared, so did my chance of getting most of the cash I was owed. Knocking on the door of a Shanklin flat and trying to prise money out of the publisher, Eric Bradburn, was not my style at all. The contacts I made, like Don Moody, Don Duval and Reg Campbell, made it all worth while, however. They made we welcome at local theatres.

The autumn of 1975 was to change my life forever. My father came home from the *County Press* with the news that two of their much respected staff, gifted sports editor Keith Newbery and deputy editor Keith Huyton, a tough Yorkshireman, with a somewhat feared reputation, were leaving to form their own local tabloid, the *Isle of Wight Weekly Post*. They were taking on their old employers head-on.

I voiced an interest and was invited to a meeting at Sandown's Fountain Inn with the two Keiths. They were looking for ideas. Did I have any? For once, I pushed myself forward. I should have done it much more in my life-time. My enthusiastic love of showbiz led to the offer of my *Stage Talk* column. My love for local sports people also gave me the chance to feature a second weekly column, the *Post Sports Personality*.

The first paper was published on November 21, 1975, and I was a regular until its sad demise in 1990. In fact, I never missed a single issue. Even on family holidays I wrote articles in hotel rooms and on the beach. Then, having a day job, as a salesman with KP McVitie's, and being a freelance evening and week-end journalist, was hard to accommodate. Whilst playing cricket for Godshill I wrote articles when we were batting. I trusted the early batsmen and they rarely let me down.

Having the support of my entire family was very important. My two children, Sean and Caroline, grew up in the company of famous stars. They just looked on them as normal people and friends. They were never overawed by meeting famous names. Sometimes a few of their friends were envious but they could never understand why. In hindsight, what experience that proved. The ability to be able to converse with so many confident and successful people was a great training ground for them. Thankfully, neither has inherited dad's initial shyness.

I'll never forget the day I went to Andover to meet Reg Presley, at the time his song *Love Is All Around* was top of the charts for Wet Wet Wet. The day started badly with a traffic jam on the Winchester by-pass. During our enforced stop came the sad news of Roy Castle's death. It had a numbing effect on both Sean and myself.

We arrived late in Andover and then could find nowhere to park. I dropped Sean outside the hotel and told him to find Reg and apologise. Within five minutes I was in the hotel and sat at the bar, like old friends, were Reg and Sean, who had a huge pint in his hand.

The *Stage Talk* days were so exciting. Dana was the first person I interviewed for the column. What a welcome she gave me. Roy Hudd once told me she was like Cinderella off-stage. How right he was. There are few, if any, nicer people in the business. Over the next fifteen years it wasn't all going to be as good as this.

The next interview – or non interview – at Sandown Pavilion was in complete contrast. It was a concert by a '60s pop star and his band. He just didn't want to know and was most unfriendly. There was also a strange smell, backstage. It certainly wasn't Craven A or Players No. 6.

December 5, 1975, was a night I'll never forget. World-famous jazz violinist Stephane Grappelli was due at the Sandown Pavilion. It was a full house and the Frenchman was in superb form. What a character, too. At that time he was well over seventy and, prior to arriving on the Island, he had to stand all the way on the Waterloo to Portsmouth train. Even so, he found time for an interview.

I was invited backstage after the show and finally bid a goodnight to Stephane as he headed for a seafront hotel. Ten minutes later he was back – and as white as a sheet. Apparently the only entrance to the hotel was through the back garden and a huge dog refused to let him through.

"These hands are so precious to me and are insured for £10,000," revealed a somewhat shaken Grappelli. He made it quite clear he had no intention of going back to that hotel. It was now after 11 o'clock on a cold December night in Sandown. Stephane looked to me for inspiration. I decided to put him in my car and drive him to Ryde. We arrived at Yelfs Hotel and were given a warm

welcome. They had a spare room. The panic was over – and there was not a dog in sight.

"Would you like to eat?" asked a very happy violinist.

Stephane Grappelli, a late night car passenger.

14

Within fifteen minutes we were sat in the Chinese restaurant just up the hill. I'd even rung home to get permission – and I think I got it. That meal was quite remarkable – not only for the great food but the hospitality and genial charm of Stephane. I heard so many stories of the *Quintette du Hot Club de France* and his wartime reflections. It turned out that Stephane's first visit to the Island had been during the war as a naval rating with the French forces. He had been a crewman aboard one of the *chasseurs* which berthed at Marvin's Yard, Cowes.

At around that time I also met the inimitable Arthur Askey. That was a real thrill. My parents had always enthralled me with stories of Arthur's eight summer seasons at Shanklin's Summer Theatre, now an amusement arcade. It happened in those days, too. That Sunshine company led the Liverpool comedian to eventual stardom. Within two summers of leaving Shanklin he was one of Britain's most famous entertainers.

One of his fans at Shanklin was David Niven, who was then living at Bembridge. Amazingly, just up the road at the Pier Theatre was another burgeoning comedy star, Tommy Trinder. There were rumours that the owners used to focus binoculars on the Summer Theatre to see how many were going in – or it could have been the other way 'round.

I learnt a lot from Arthur Pinder, who was the stage manager for Arthur's shows. His father, Powis Pinder, ran the theatre, which had been built from old seaplane sheds at Bembridge. Arthur Pinder lived at Niton until his death.

Meeting Arthur Askey for a few minutes finally realised an ambition of mine. A week or two later he actually wrote me a letter, complimenting me on the accuracy of an article I'd written on his old days at Shanklin.

In 1998 I finally caught up with his daughter, Anthea, who went to school at Upper Chine. I went to her home in Angmering to interview Anthea for Isle of Wight Radio and the *County Press*. It was to tie in with the closing of her old Island school. Despite being ill with cancer, Anthea bravely undertook our interview and was in sparkling form. It seemed to be a kind of therapy, talking about her affection for the Island. I was so glad I went and that she was really determined to do it.

Anthea actually made her acting début at the Town Hall, Ventnor, in the professional summer repertory company. Dad even came down to see the play. She had been thrilled to get time off school. Anthea went on to work with stars like David Nixon. Her stories about Upper Chine included finding an under-ground tunnel that took them under the road and into a garden full of fruit, and being made to stand on a stool for several hours, after being seen eating ice cream on a Sunday afternoon in Shanklin's Regent Street.

There was bad news in March 1999 when Anthea lost her brave fight. The last time I spoke to her, on the 'phone, we had a few laughs. Her dream of coming back to Upper Chine, when it became an hotel, was never to be.

The late Jack Nightingale, from Shanklin, one of the Island's great charac-ters, played host to Jack Warner. The invitation to go and meet such a famous star at Jack and Elaine's home was so unexpected. We had a tea party in the garden and I learnt much about his career and PC George Dixon. There were endless memories of *The Huggetts*, Garrison Theatre and, of course, "Mind my bike!", his original catchphrase long before "Evenin' all!".

Many professional actors and entertainers have settled on the Island. In more recent times these have included Michael Sheard, Kenneth Kendall, Reginald Marsh, Jack Douglas and Celia Imrie. Back in the '60s and '70s Barney Powell was another. He lived at Luccombe and ran his famous Shanklin Emporium. By night he was a theatre and cabaret performer.

Barney readily admitted to being a "warmer upper". A performer who supported the star names. He once described himself as like the man who passed the ball to Georgie Best. The bill-toppers were so pleased to have him on their shows. Barney never failed to win over the audience. When the big names came to the Island they always went to look up Barney. Dick Emery was a regular, and so was Tommy Trinder.

When Roy Hudd topped the bill at Shanklin Theatre, Barney was on the same bill. I shall never forget Roy's delight at watching him work for the first time. Barney always told me he knew Bruce Forsyth and the TV star, then equally unknown, working with young Barney at the Windmill Theatre, gave him a pair of his dancing shoes. Long after Barney had sadly passed away, Bruce confirmed the story to me.

The Ponda Rosa, particularly in the '70s, was a thriving roadhouse and cabaret club at Ashey, near Ryde. The Green family brought over some of the biggest names in the business. Rumour has it that over 500 crammed in to see the Wurzels, at the height of their fame. I can remember many

Roy Hudd, bill-topper at Shanklin.

standing on chairs. Clive Green was a shrewd cabaret-booker, always on the lookout for a good deal. The Ponda's Saturday night dinner dances were extremely popular, especially when acts like Patsy Peters were on view.

Not long after Jim Davidson had come second to Roger De Courcey (more of him later) on *New Faces* he still honoured his booking for Clive's Saturday night cabaret. How times have changed! At that time Jim was a somewhat nervous character and certainly not the world's most confident performer. He was only too pleased to be interviewed – a policy he was to drastically change in later years. I have never forgiven him for refusing to do an interview in memory of a mutual friend, who had died of cancer.

Jim Davidson, young and innocent, at the Ponda Rosa.

The story begins in the '80s when I was invited to the Portsmouth Guildhall by Jim's tour manager, the lovely Peter Brown, to interview the comedian. It had all been set up. When I arrived Jim was in real trouble. He'd cried-off the night before and was still struggling with 'flu. Mike Osman had been brought in to take over some of his solo spots. I took one look at Jim and promptly said I would not consider interviewing him for one moment. That was the least of his needs. He was so grateful and vowed to do another at a later date. Peter Brown would arrange it.

Within a year Peter Brown had died. I'd first met him when he was a company manager for David Essex. Nothing was too much trouble for Peter. So many were saddened by his early death. I knew Peter was keen for Jim to undertake that postponed interview. So, a few months later, I wrote to Jim suggesting we might do the promised interview in Peter's memory. After two attempts and no response, I gave up the idea. I had proof that he had received my letters. When Jim Davidson was at the Ponda we almost had to talk him into going on stage, he was so nervous.

How different Bruce Forsyth, a real star, was to prove in 1998. More of that in a few chapters time.

CHAPTER FIVE

OLLIE'S TROUSERS & ROGER'S NOOKIE

ONE EVENING in 1980 I was at Wootton interviewing Newport cricketer Mike Blackman for my *Post Sports Personality* column. The 'phone rang and it was the in-house photographer from the Ponda Rosa. Oliver Reed had turned up and had just dropped his trousers. It could be a story? With Mike Blackman not having a reputation for dropping his, I quickly finished his life story and headed for Ashey. When I arrived Ollie was in quite a state – which was no real surprise.

He would not have known if his pants were up or down. One or two local ladies seemed to have been glad they were there. In one of my better judgements, I decided the time was just not right to request an interview with Oliver. Two nights earlier he'd scared me out of my wits, watching him in a late night horror movie. I hadn't planned to be in one. There had also been positive proof, over the years, that he was partial to a little press bashing – in more ways than one. My claim to Ollie Reed fame is that I actually stood five yards away from him, wanting an interview. Luckily, he didn't know.

I did file a story for the *Post* which was much appreciated by his close Island pal Gus Gustar, the former entertainment's manager at Warner's Puckpool. I know he sent Mr Reed a copy – and he loved it. Now they have both passed on.

Roy Castle was very popular at the Ponda Rosa and made many marvellous cabaret appearances, which were always sell-outs. During the early days of his career he'd worked with a very funny performer called Bob Muir, in a summer season at Cleveleys. I had something of a scoop when the self-same Bob turned up at the Ponda. He was now living on the Isle of Wight. Watching those two going through an old routine, backstage, was so funny.

Sylvia Thorley, the local agent, held an early showcase at this venue. It was a great night and one of the acts, a young teenager called Louise English, stole the evening. She was nothing short of sensational. I gave her great reviews in both the *Post* and *The Stage*. A few years later, after she was a regular on Benny Hill's TV shows and had starred in the West End production of *Me and My Girl*, Louse admitted, on a holiday to the Island, that it was those early write-ups of mine that actually stopped her leaving the business. It would have been a tragedy if she had.

There were so many great nights at the Ponda. They all came – Charlie Williams, Frankie Vaughan, Mike and Bernie Winters, Billy J. Kramer, Peter Noone, Acker Bilk, Lonnie Donegan and Marty Wilde. There were also a few hen and stag nights. On a hen night I turned up to talk to a pop singer who was on the bill. I had a somewhat hostile reception from the male strippers who were worried that the press were in. When I saw them I was worried for another reason and quickly left. I would have felt safer with female strippers.

Once at a Newport Football Club dinner dance, arranged by their flamboyant chairman Roy Dew, Alan Simpson was the guest speaker. What a scriptwriter, too. He wrote *Hancock* and *Steptoe*, with his colleague Ray Galton. They both met while patients at the old Ventnor Sanatorium.

I've always thrived on scoops, which are basically stories that you've beaten everyone else to or have been given exclusively. The latter can often be derived from having a trusted reputation. Over the years I've seen many things I shouldn't have, particularly in theatres, dressing rooms and hotels. Those secrets remain safe with me.

Through my long-term contacts with local musicians like Doug Watson, Tim Marshall and Andy Skelton, I was given the nudge nudge, wink wink tip that their group, Brother, were appearing in a heat of TV's *New Faces*. What a gem of a story! A few favours were called in and they agreed to tell no-one.

New Faces! – Keep it quiet, lads, I want a scoop.
Brother and Kite within a week.
Andy Skelton, Doug Watson and Tim Marshall.

It worked like a dream and the very day before their television debut, *Stage Talk* had a marvellous exclusive. They won, and the following week also won an all-winners show – under their new name of Kite. Eventually they became the top group of the entire series, after doing so well in the Grand Final.

Between their appearances on *New Faces*, the boys were forced to change their name, due to another chart group having a similar name. Later I was to interview that group, Brothers, at the Memorial Hall, Freshwater. Back to Kite, for a second. If only their management had been more effective – they had so much potential and even impressed the hard-headed Mickie Most.

If only he had taken them on. Being such talented musicians, all three have made a good living from the music business, as individuals. Andy's later emergence in an Abba tribute band must surely have been purely for the money. I still rate him the most gifted musician/songwriter the Island has ever produced.

Patience has long been an important virtue for any journalist. Quite often you can spend some considerable time just hanging around theatres or holiday centres. When Reg Campbell, the former Medina Council amenities officer, invited me to Little Canada to interview Joe Loss, I couldn't get there quick enough. I needn't have hurried. Joe was asleep and I waited five hours for a five-minute interview. Luckily, he was a quick talker.

During that same year another famous bandleader, Eric Delaney, was rumoured to be resident at the Warner's Woodside Bay holiday complex. En route to the now defunct woodland centre I spotted a van with Eric's logo on the side. Hastily I followed it through Wootton and down the unmade road towards the centre. It took longer than expected.

Eric's van was involved in a minor accident as two vehicles tried to pass in one of the narrowest parts of the bumpy lane. Thankfully, only the paintwork was slightly damaged. I duly followed the van and within minutes was in earnest conversation with the great drummer. Eric's a wonderful and genial character who does a lot of good work for the hard of hearing. If you are partly deaf in any way, go along to one of his concerts and you won't have a problem anymore. What a showman! Pardon?

I returned to Woodside Bay two years later to try and interview Roger De Courcey, who had won *New Faces* with his hand up Nookie Bear. Roger can be one of the rudest men in show business. At that time, I wasn't aware of that. He did agree to an interview, which I now realise must have been a fluke, but was none to happy with the photo idea. Neither *Post* photographer Chris Thwaites nor myself could persuade him into putting Nookie in the driver's seat of his Range Rover, as if the bear was driving. In the end Roger insisted on a straight head and shoulders shot. It wasn't until later that night that I was discreetly told he'd recently been banned from driving. That was Roger – not Nookie.

That particular night during the whole of Roger's act a punter was playing the fruit machine. You could see the ventriloquist, sorry about the slight exaggeration, seething with anger and Nookie got more insulting as he continually swore at the holidaymaker. Eventually the message got through.

Over the years I've been so embarrassed for professional entertainers at certain local holiday centres. So often they are shown no respect at all from mindless punters. It was nothing to see a woman walk in front of a cabaret artist, wheeling a pushchair. Youngsters have walked up to well-known comedians and offered them chips. Midnight cabaret stars are on a hiding to nothing.

The holidaymakers have been in the room for around six hours to get the best seats. With the heat, noise and booze forming a lethal combination, the poor late night entertainer struggles to survive. I once saw a superb comedian, Jeff Stevenson, who went on to host TV's *Jumble* game show, shorten his act by half. England had just been knocked out of the World Cup and no-one wanted to laugh that night. Most of these incidents are restricted to the more down-market holiday centres.

Back to Roger De Courcey. That was the only time I've ever interviewed him. During the '80s, at Sandown Pavilion, he promised me an interview and told me to be at the stage door at 5 p.m. He was there but completely ignored me and walked off the pier. Just a year or two later I wrote a friendly letter to his agent to ask if Roger could spare a few minutes during his cabaret visit to Warner's Yarmouth. Back came the reply stating Mr De Courcey was not interested in any way.

Ironically, he 'died' on stage that night as he visibly struggled to make any impact. I've never tried since – and never will. Thankfully, people like him are a minority in the world of show business.

The summer of '77 at Shanklin Theatre introduced Peter Cleall from television's *Please Sir!*, as the principal star in their repertory season. He was helpful in every way and so was the company manager Michael Boothe, who had family ties on the Island. He also appeared in the productions. Michael and John Newman, the director, became good friends of ours.

We did enjoy Michael's long friendship and were heartbroken when he was later murdered in London. That tragedy was almost certainly due to him being a member of the gay fraternity. It was a probable case of gay bashing. Over the years we have met so many showbiz people who have enjoyed a similar lifestyle and have always found them so likeable, helpful and courteous. Many have given me memorable interviews.

During that Shanklin summer season there were also a few Sunday concerts, including one featuring actor Dennis Waterman, a much under-rated rock singer. That year the then *Sweeney* star had released his superb début album *Downwind of Angels*. Dennis surprised quite a few with his vocal quality and went on to enjoy a couple of hit singles. Such a nice guy, too. I found him refreshingly shy in those days.

Sylvia 'Smiler' Thorley has often put stories my way. This Bonchurch agent has so many friends in the entertainment business. At her initial request I was invited to the Cliff Tops Hotel, Shanklin, to meet a new singing trio, Beverley Rainbow. They turned out to be the daughters of the world famous Beverley Sisters, who had conquered America in the '50s. Then such a rare feat for a British act.

After our interview, their first as Beverley Rainbow, I spotted this famous couple coming into the room. It was Joy and Billy Wright, the parents of two of the girls. Joy I'd seen so many times on television and Billy, her husband, was one of my first real soccer heroes. I remember going to Fratton Park to watch the great Wolves side.

What a thrill in those days to have seen Billy and Bert Williams in the same team. Now here were Billy Wright and me having a cup of coffee. He was a real gentleman who willingly agreed to an interview. I was so sad when he died during the '90s. Joy subsequently paid him a most moving tribute on one of my radio shows.

Teddie, Joy and Babs have long been good family friends, having watched and enjoyed Sean and Caroline growing up. When they made their live début on *John Hannam Meets* they almost didn't make it, having got lost on the way

*Mr and Mrs Billy Wright
and Beverley Rainbow at the Cliff Tops, Shanklin.*

from the Swainston Manor Hotel to the studio. Many times I've acted as their unpaid roadie at gigs. The kisses at the end were ample reward.

Talking of late arrivals, ask Ray McVay! This famous bandleader who was the king of *Come Dancing* for many years asked to come live on my radio show to plug his forthcoming Glenn Miller tribute show. They drove down from London and actually arrived whilst the news was on, with all of two minutes to spare.

Whenever the 'phone rings I always anticipate a scoop – or at least a good story or an interview promise. Most times it's probably Ron Sheppard. Ron, who has a direct line to me, from all over the world, has come up with some great ideas and interviews. Thanks Ron – and he's a good sport.

One summer's night a call came in from nearby Wroxall. It was a mother saying a famous film star had actually turned up for her daughter's birthday party. It was hard to digest and did I recognise the voice? Within minutes I was at the party with an early *Post* photographer, Alan Plummer, who was a neighbour.

It was true but I'm not so sure Sarah Douglas, from movies like *The People That Time Forgot*, *Superman 1*, *Superman 2* and *Conon The Destroyer* plus the American hit TV series, *Falcon Crest*, was

*Sarah Douglas – from
Hollywood to a
Wroxall birthday party.*

22

too pleased. For some reason Alan Plummer was not her favourite person. It must have been the poised camera. Sarah quickly warmed to us and we pulled a few crackers and wore funny hats – and got our story. Sarah, a Hollywood starlet, was the real cracker.

When our daughter Caroline was born in April 1978 there were obviously great family celebrations. My wonderful late mother-in-law, Peggy, came to Godshill to look after Sean and myself. Heather was still in hospital, as both our youngsters were born via cæsarean section. How could I keep my *Weekly Post* column going and visit St Mary's every night? Enter the man who made it all possible.

Leslie Evans was the manager of the Farringford Hotel, at Freshwater Bay. We had dined there on a few occasions with showbiz friends. At this particular time they had a Decca Radar conference, with celebrated after-dinner speakers every night. With meticulous timing I left the hospital every night and went home via Freshwater Bay. In three consecutive nights I interviewed Sir Brian Rix, Cardew Robinson and newsreader Peter Woods. That was three weeks *Stage Talk* in three nights.

The first famous star that Caroline ever met was Max Boyce. During Heather's pregnancy she had problems with blood pressure and was forced to take more rest than normal. Through this, she missed meeting Max on his first-ever Island gig, at Sandown. Max sent Heather a message and signed photo, as she was not well enough to go to the show. On his next visit, we took Caroline along to the Cliff Tops, to prove that it really was worth Heather missing that first concert – and Max sat the proof on his knee. He made a real fuss of Caroline. Oggy, oggy, oggy!

Oggy, Oggy, Oggy.
Caroline and Uncle Max.

There are numerous other memories from the home of Tennyson. A marvellous dinner with Ted Rogers and his wife Marion. They even provided our baby sitters, Marion's parents. What service. Dining with a famous star can be like living in a goldfish bowl, with so many people trying to steal a look at the personality. One night, earlier that summer, I was having a drink with Ted in the Islander Bar, on Sandown Pier, when a local yob came up and gave him a lot of abuse. It was completely without provocation. I was more embarrassed than Ted. He took it all so well.

Leslie Evans at the Farringford was an excellent contact but on one occasion his good intentions were brought to an abrupt end by actor Tom Conti. Les 'phoned to say Tom was staying at the hotel and would certainly do an interview that evening. I nipped along the Military Road and waited patiently, with my nervous excitement just about under control.

Suddenly Les appeared and stammered that Tom would not do the interview that night. It was his social time and he'd been filming all day. Sometimes Tom was swept off by helicopter after a day's shooting for other engagements in London. I fully accepted the situation and Tom came in to see me and invited me to their Niton film set the following day, with the promise of an interview. He kept his word on the set of the television drama *Blade On The Feather*, filmed at Mirables, on the Niton Undercliff.

That production, made just after the Blunt spy revelations, also starred the legendary Donald Pleasence. He was also up for an interview and appeared in his dressing gown and led me into a creepy old room in this fascinating

Donald Pleasence and film crew at Mirables, Niton.

country house. For a few moments I thought of *Halloween*. Donald had scared me in that movie. He stayed for around fifteen minutes and then stressed he must go and learn his lines. He was filming in ten minutes.

It was quite a day and during my taped conversation with Donald, Denholm Elliott walked through. It was a good day for star-spotting. I watched several takes of one of Donald's major scenes before he sneaked away for a quiet drink at the St Lawrence Inn.

24

CHAPTER SIX

TITTERS ON THE MENU

DOES NO always mean no? In my experience the answer is simply no – well, it was in the case of Tony Blackburn. He came to the Island for a roadshow and was booked in at the Shanklin Hotel. Having prepared in advance, I'd written to Tony at the BBC and received a favourable answer. When I arrived at the requested time of 5.30 p.m., the hotel receptionist rang his room and I overheard the conversation in which Tony said he wouldn't do it and didn't wish to be disturbed at all. I swallowed any resentment and still vowed to be a Tony Blackburn fan. I have always remembered his launch programme for Radio 1.

I'd arrived home a little disappointed and was eating my fish and chips when the 'phone rang. My wife answered and excitedly said "It's Tony Blackburn for you". Tony had rung up to apologise profusely and stated that he hadn't realised it was me at the hotel. Apparently all that day he'd been hounded by another local media person and thought it was him in the hotel reception. Would I like to go down to the hotel the following morning and he would see me. True to his word, he did everything that was asked.

Many years later during a Cowes Week gig for Isle of Wight Radio he came in and appeared on my chat show. Tony is one of national radio's great professionals. There are few as good as him, today. I was also more than surprised that on his regular private visits to the Island he had actually listened to my show and knew all about it.

Syd Lawrence had been to Sandown Pavilion many times but would never do an interview. In desperation I wrote a pleading letter to Bob Marr, his manager, to see if Syd would have a change of heart. It worked and he joined in the spirit of the long-term chase by giving an interview and posing for some fun pictures. I played his trumpet and he took the notes. Mind you, he'd never heard the like of the ones I played.

Saturday, September 16th, 1978, was an historic night at the Sandown Pavilion.

Ace showbiz reporter Syd Lawrence and a new trumpet star. It certainly made my hair grow.

September 16th, 1978 – the night Mike and Bernie Winters finally parted.

Sadly, it was the last night that Mike and Bernie Winters ever appeared together. They had formed their comedy double act in the early '50s and were even on shows like *Six-Five Special*. As a live act they were quite superb and so much funnier than in their rather ordinary television appearances. That summer, which pioneered the way for star name holiday seasons, they made thousands of fans on the Island. The brothers also broke all box office records – before the arrival of James Tarbuck, the following summer.

Clearly at the Pavilion all was not well with Mike and Bernie. They were just not getting on, had separate dressing rooms and were virtually not speaking off-stage. They did get together for their last-ever interview, which was published in *Stage Talk* on the eve of their last show together. Mike went off to America and Bernie went solo. He came back to Sandown several times and was always good company. We became good friends and had a few laughs. The secret can now be revealed – there were at least four different dogs who took the rôle of Schnorbitz.

Gene Pitney came to Sandown on November 26 of the same year. What a coup for Joyce Coleman, booking this American superstar for a one-nighter. The announcement had been another *Stage Talk* scoop and 1,000 tickets were sold in just three hours. Gene, whose publicist had once been Robin Britten from Bembridge, would not do any interviews. I was prepared to wait.

The opportunity came fully eighteen years later, at the Guildhall, Portsmouth. In the media business it's definitely a case of who you know. My good mate Bobby Crush was the support act for Gene's '96 British tour. Bob spoke up for me and just hours before the Portsmouth gig I was invited over to meet Gene Pitney. That long and patient wait was worth it. I think he may have admired my tenacity. Gene was very hospitable and what a unique singing voice.

In September of 1980 John Gould, from Shanklin, invited me down to the old Ryde Airport site to interview a brand new band, with three locals, who had just made their first single for Polydor. One of the great fascinations of my life has been to monitor the success of young Islanders, whether it be in music, industry, sport or commerce. More of that later.

On this autumn morning my potential target was a band called Level 42. Mark King and the Gould brothers, Phil and Boon, had all played on the local scene. Phil was a good friend of mine and we'd often listened to demo music tapes at his home in Green Lane, Shanklin. I can remember when he first played me tracks by M, on which he was featured on drums. Phil was also in that original Brother line-up and had played in the Ponda Rosa band.

Level 42 – their first-ever interview, at Ryde's Carousel Club.

I sensed another scoop. The first interview in the world with Level 42. From those early records, I knew they would go on to become such a mega band. Their attitude was perfect and they had all the ambition, confidence and drive that was needed in such a cut throat industry. The boys' subsequent success warmed the hearts of so many Islanders. We must not forget Mike

27

Lindup, the only mainlander in the band. He also had such a great influence on their music.

Sadly, not all locals can cope with the success of fellow Islanders. Over the years I've encountered a fair amount of envy and jealousy from certain quarters, albeit a minority. It's an attitude I've always found difficult to understand. Why enjoy knocking an Islander who has broken away to enjoy nationwide or even worldwide acclaim?

Mark King, subsequently, was a generous host at both Gurnard Marsh and Wootton. Phil invited me to his old Ryde pad and even gave me his copy of their very first Polydor album, which is still my personal favourite of all their records. When Mark kicked off a charity football match at St George's Park, Newport, in 1990, he willingly agreed to a spot on *John Hannam Meets*. That eventually materialised in September 1998 – but, once again, the wait was worth it. I doubt if Mark could ever surpass that two-hour chat show performance. It was repeated by public demand and there were requests for tapes from all over the world.

Level 42's performance at Ryde Arena, in 1991, was one of the great all-time moments in the history of the Island's live music scene. There were over three thousand at the concert. In March of 1999 he came back to Ryde Theatre as a solo performer, with his new band, and again provided marvellous entertainment. Fans even came from America and France just to see it. It was almost a case of full circle. In his new line-up were another three Islanders, Mark, brother Nathan and Trevor Smith.

From the days of *Variety Bandbox* on the good old Light Programme, I'd been an ardent fan of Frankie Howerd. This comedy genius had not always been the toast of British audiences. On occasions his popularity had waned quite dramatically. *That Was The Week That Was* and *Up Pompeii!* had almost re-invented Francis Howerd. Then he became a cult figure with many young people, particularly on university campuses.

Frankie came to Sandown Pavilion for a summer season in 1980. What was Frank really like? He was such a great hit, on stage, except with a friend of mine who even rang me up to say how much he hadn't enjoyed Frankie on the pier. He was in the minority.

Then came a much more welcome yet unexpected call from the great man himself,

Even Frankie Howerd read 'Stage Talk'.

28

inviting Heather and myself out to a late night dinner at the Culver Haven. We were told to meet Frankie and his party after the Pavilion show. The line-up for that round table dinner was Frankie, his manager Dennis, pianist Madame Dixon, plus Heather and me.

Initially we all sat in the bar area and the atmosphere was somewhat subdued, and that's an understatement. At least I was there. Twenty years earlier I wouldn't have been able to accept the invite. Embarrassment would have got the better of me. How could I now get Frankie going? He had told me to call him Frank. Then came an idea. I knew he was a great tennis lover and now was the chance to put it to the test.

I can remember starting a conversation with these words: "Frank, I thought of you on Saturday afternoon when I saw that marvellous Wimbledon final between Borg and McEnroe." With that he burst into enthusiastic conversation and it was nearly two hours before he stopped.

It was a night to savour. The guest of Frankie Howerd – and the titters just never stopped. I said very little. That was deliberate. Why stop a legend when he's in full cry? Frank remarked how he liked my suit. I suggested that I hadn't been quite sure how to dress for dinner with him. Frankie knew exactly what I meant. He never had that Burton's window touch.

My wife answered the most questions, all from Frank. What was I like indoors? What did I eat? What are his bad habits? Then he stared right at me and exclaimed: "John, do you ever worry about dying?" I had to admit I had never ever thought about it.

As we left the Culver Haven at about 1.30 a.m., it was a wonderful moonlit morning over Sandown Bay. Frank was still in full flow and enquired if I knew anything about stars. I reminded him I'd been lucky to interview so many but was way off his train of thought. With his hand placed around my shoulder he introduced me to The Great Bear and other heavenly formations.

There will never be another Frankie Howerd. That horrendous Easter week-end, in April 1992, when both Frankie and Benny Hill died, was a double tragedy from which British show business has never recovered. They were true stars.

We had been on a family holiday when Benny Hill made a surprise visit to Ryde Pavilion to greet old friends Billy Whittaker and Mimi Law. There was compensation when, in 1989, I was invited to an end-of-season lunch party at Shanklin's Lincoln Hotel, by Sylvia Thorley. 'Smiler' had hinted that Benny Hill might just attend. A few years earlier two of Sylvia's local dancers, Lesley Young and Cheryl Mortimore, had become Hill's Angels and appeared on many of his television shows.

I arrived and there, sat amongst a bevy of lovely young ladies, was the marvellous Benny Hill. He was at his happiest surrounded by pretty girls. Who wouldn't be? Don't answer that. On this autumn lunch-time Benny was in the perfect mood to be interviewed and there was an attentive audience. Amazingly, the Southampton *Evening Echo* could never tie up an interview

29

with one of that city's favourite residents. Mind you, some of the national press had made Benny more than a little suspicious of the media. In the end, the *Echo* was happy to take my Benny Hill interview and turned it into a full page spread with colour pictures. They were happy and so was Benny. I was just thrilled to have met him.

I must admit a love for pantomime. Even now on my annual pilgrimage to review south coast shows for *The Stage*, I can still be caught shouting out with all the kids. Being in a panto full-house can be so exhilarating. Some of the lovely 'ladies' are intriguing, too. Keep reading.

When Burden and Moran came to the Island during the late '70s for a summer season, I was in need of a fun story for the *Weekly Post*. Then in a flash of inspiration I wondered if even I could get away with being a dame.

There was no doubt it would take quite a lot of work. Roger and Maurice were game to give it a try. Chris Thwaites just couldn't believe it. He was there to photograph every move. It seemed to take hours. The make-up was layered on, beauty spots arrived from a box and false eyelashes were added. Even the dress fitted – although I seemed a little flat chested.

All 'girls' together – one has written this book.

It was all over and the great test was set in motion. On the same bill was one of the world's greatest ventriloquists, Arthur Worsley, who had even appeared on the *Ed Sullivan Show* with Elvis Presley. Arthur and his wife Audrey had become family friends. He was ushered into the dressing room and looked puzzled. "Do I know you? Your face does look familiar," queried

Arthur. He really had no idea. The dame in me had fooled an old pro. It also fooled over 20,000 readers.

Another self-inflicted story I did for the *Weekly Post* came in the autumn of 1980. Like so many youngsters who were lucky enough to be into popular music at the concept of the Elvis Presley phenomenon, I always wanted to be a singer. There might have been some hint of promising vocal chords when I joined the choir at the East Cowes Methodist church and even sang solo at Christmas concerts. After my voice broke I didn't sing another solo until September 1980 – and that was in East Cowes, this time behind the closed doors of a York Avenue recording studio.

I suppose I always wanted to make a record. This eventually came to the notice of a few pals from local pop groups – Rod Gammons, who went on to become a chart record producer, Tim Marshall and Andy Skelton, both of Kite fame, backing singer Fiona Groves and studio owner Tim Muncaster.

The plot was hatched and I spent over five hours recording three songs. Those chosen to suit my limited vocal talents and range were *Poor Little Fool*, *Things* and *Shoo Doo Fu Fu Ooh!* I couldn't sing. The boys weren't worried. Many had made the charts with a similar problem – and still do. This was not a commercial venture or an attempt at an early brand of Brit pop.

One of my favourite local radio presenters is Richard Cartridge from Radio Solent. That view has never changed – although he's certainly moved stations a few times. I sent Richard a copy of the tracks at Solent for pure fun. He loved it and invited myself and Tim Marshall over to his *Happening Now* morning show at their South Western House studio. We actually followed Sweet Substitute.

The 'Weekly Post's' mystery singer – and Solent's Richard Cartridge was a fan.

31

It was an enjoyable experience and – wait for it – one or two 'phoned up to try and buy it. Luckily, so far, none have escaped. Directly after Richard's show I reversed the rôles and interviewed him for my *Stage Talk* column.

There were also local night club links with the best of the three tracks, *Poor Little Fool*. The build-up in the *Post* as to who this new singer could be was heightened when six of the top local DJ's had taped copies to play in their clubs and mobile discos. They were Dave Cannon (Ryde Queen), Den Bunce (Bogey's), Paul Grimes (Babalu), Gerry and Pete (Rupert's), Dave Cass and Jean Paul. Who is the mystery singer?

I had an embarrassing experience during the Gary Glitter one-nighter at Colwell Bay's Fort Warden holiday centre. The DJ for the evening was JP of Vectis Sound Systems. He actually played it to the hundreds of punters. Luckily, I managed to answer a call of nature at that precise moment.

Let's stay on the subject of Gary Glitter. On that particular night I enquired about the possibility of an interview with Mr Glitter, who had just been declared bankrupt. Back came the reply, from the roadie, that he'd just thrown out a *Sun* reporter. Not to be brushed aside I sent back a business card with a scribbled note on the back, claiming I was only interested in his pop career, not his business or private life.

They promised an interview – and kept their word. It was a trifle later than expected. Gary played the superstar rôle and kept me waiting until 2 a.m. I can remember leaving the centre at 2.30 a.m. With a day job as well, in those days, I only had around three hours sleep.

When he came back to the Island, in the '90s, Gary Glitter would not do any interviews. Not even Alex Dyke could conjure up an interview with his great hero. That hurried early morning ten minutes is still the only interview Glitter ever did on the Island. It's unlikely he'll appear here any more.

Peters and Lee made some wonderfully commercial records, and first came here during 1980 to headline at the Sandown Pavilion. I knew my good pal Wally Malston was a friend of Lennie Peters and he agreed to put a word in for me. When I arrived at Sandown their unhelpful roadie hinted that if they knew I was coming it would be okay. If not, he would not let me in to see them.

The mention of Wally's much respected name was the password needed. As I walked in Lennie remarked: "You must be John, Wally's friend". I was certainly made so welcome by Lennie and Di. It was like a meeting of long-lost friends, such was the warmth of their hospitality. We were to meet up on several more occasions after that. For a period of years they disbanded Peters and Lee. Di enjoyed a solo summer season at Sandown. Then they re-formed.

Ten years after that Sandown début I met Lennie for the very last time, at Warner's Bembridge Coast Hotel. He was not too well at that time. They still wanted to do an interview and I also doubled as Lennie's personal assistant for an hour or two. That meant lighting a cigarette for the first time in my life and looking after his whisky. They were such a brilliant act. I was so saddened by Lennie's death.

One night I went in search of Britain's most celebrated political failure – Screaming Lord Sutch. I'd never met David but knew a lot about his career and had met many top stars who had actually once played in his backing band, like Paul Nicholas. The venue was Nodes Point, St Helens, and, as usual, manager Chris Norman was the perfect host. I was standing at the bar drinking Coke and assumed I was just among holidaymakers. Suddenly Chris came back and introduced me to the guy stood next to me, Screaming Lord Sutch. He was in a sports jacket – and I'd never seen him without his top hat, wig and coffin. Sutch was one of many showbiz deaths in 1999.

The month was March 1991 and, purely by accident, I rumbled a burgeoning romance at the Shanklin Theatre. Keith Chegwin was over for a children's show and, being the nice guy he is, he agreed to a Saturday morning interview at the theatre. During our chat the door slowly opened and I instantly felt a hot flush – and it wasn't shyness, this time. In walked Maggie Philbin. In winter, on Saturday mornings, I joined my youngsters to watch *Swap Shop*, just to see Maggie. It was nothing more than a forty-year-old dad's crush on a TV star.

They were quick off the mark, too. Keith insisted he'd just run into Maggie, who was spending the week-end on the Island. I bought it, of course. Several months later a tabloid exclusively revealed their love affair. There you go – I could have made a fortune.

The following year I suddenly met someone else I'd fallen in love with many years before Maggie Philbin. It was Sooty. Matthew Corbett willingly undertook an interview at the Ryde Pavilion. Then I noticed a familiar face in the back row of the theatre. It was Sooty's creator, Harry Corbett. At that time Harry was living in Bournemouth and helping Matthew out on a few occasions. In Dorset he also did a few hotel shows of his own. He actually told me a very sad story. At one Bournemouth hotel the children were told Sooty was coming to entertain them. When Harry duly arrived, with his invention, one little boy locked himself in the toilet and refused to come out until the real Sooty man came along.

I was quite intrigued to see Sooty, many years later, in the 1998/99 Mayflower panto in Southampton. He's a very clever bear, too. Much more than people realise. As well as appearing in *Goldilocks and the Three Bears*, Sooty was also on stage in his own London West End Christmas show. How do they do that? Izzy wizzy – there's now a Sooty look-a-like. He'll be on *Stars In Their Eyes* next!

CHAPTER SEVEN

RISING STARS & A GRATEFUL PETE

I'VE NEVER been able to come to terms with the rip-offs in show business, particularly when groups come to the Island with only one original member or quite often none at all. The '60s and '70s bands are some of the worst offenders.

When Peter Brennen, a local impresario, put on Paper Lace at St George's Park, Newport, I didn't recognise any of the group. None had visited Nodes Point in the '70s, when Paper Lace undertook a one-nighter. How could I check out their authenticity? When the interview time arrived it was not difficult to realise none were originals. Surely they must be impostors? On stage, groups often refer to hits as songs that are very special to us. Very crafty.

It gets worse. There have been at least two Boney M groups in existence, and the same goes for the Bay City Rollers and Bucks Fizz, with carefully worded descriptions. Mike Pender split from the original Searchers to form his own Mike Pender's Searchers and John McNally and Frankie Allen weren't too pleased. They are still in the Searchers – and great guys they are, too. The Ivy League and Amen Corner regularly come to the Island and neither have any original members at all. Herman's Hermits tour without Peter Noone, and how can you have Slade without Noddy Holder?

Another irritating habit by some performers is to cut their act short in order to catch an earlier ferry home to the mainland. Some even mention this on stage, which is the kiss of death. Once I remember Showaddywaddy being off the Sandown Pier before most of the audience.

Picking out young performers for potential stardom is always a fascinating gamble. I've certainly been proved right on a few occasions and way off course in others. Luck has always proved such a major player in reaching star status. So many of my guests have illustrated that.

During the John Redgrave era at the Sandown Pavilion, he brought a young unknown impressionist for an early season resident show. At that time his name was much smaller than the date – although his father, Bill Nankeville, had been a world-class middle-distance runner. That was soon to change.

Bobby Davro had all the potential and talent needed for stardom. Many a night we'd have a few laughs in the dressing room. It was not instant success for him at Sandown. His material was so quick and clever, particularly his University Challenge skit, it went completely over the heads of

An unknown Bobby Davro, Sandown Pavilion, 1981.

the blue rinse brigade. I did work hard that season in promoting young Mr Davro and it proved worth it. Bob has never forgotten that.

Just a few years later, in 1985, I went to see Jimmy Cricket in a Sunday concert at Sandown. Later I'll reveal two great local stories from his stay on the Island.

On that particular Sunday date was a young entertainer called Brian Conley, who did a little fire eating, singing and some brilliant comedy. I nipped backstage during the interval to meet him, following his first-half spot. That surprised him. "A press man coming to see me! I'm only the supporting act," stressed Brian. I told him he'd be a star, one day.

A week or two later he sent me a letter from Weymouth, where he was in summer season, thanking me for my interest and confidence. I've still got the letter.

I've certainly shed a few tears since then, purely with happiness. Brian has

I told him he'd become a star. Brian Conley and J.H.

become such a major British star. He can do anything – comedy, pantomime, West End plays and musicals, TV situation comedy, and record great vocal albums.

When *Jolson* came to Southampton I wrote for an interview, which was turned down by the production company. The next day I wrote a personal letter to Brian Conley and had an instant reply to join him backstage. That initial 1985 friendship has certainly continued. Once on a family holiday to Great Yarmouth, Brian was appearing in the resort. We had a dressing room invite and four guest seats arranged by him. My two youngsters were in heaven.

Andrew O'Connor breezed into Sandown Pavilion during the summer of '85 and was an instant hit. A few years earlier he'd been a raw beginner in a Medina Theatre pantomime. This time you could see stardom written all over him. Within a few years from that Nick Thomas local season, he was hosting television game shows, writing scripts for other shows and starring in top West End musicals like *Me and My Girl*. The last time I saw him, starring in *Barnum*, it was nice to see fame had not gone to his head.

In some small way I hope a few of my write-ups and interviews may have helped Islanders in their pursuit for fame and success. Quite a few have confirmed my initial confidence in their ability. Names that spring to mind include Sandown DJ Bill Padley. When he was on the Radio Victory breakfast show I once travelled over to see how he put it together. Since then he's become a very successful record producer, songwriter, with the *Top Of The Pops 2* theme to his credit, and broadcaster.

Totland's Clare Bonsu was one of several young Island hopefuls who blossomed from local dancing schools. It was a real pleasure to write the first-ever feature on her dreams and aspirations. The picture on Colwell seafront certainly turned a few heads. With West End appearances in *Miss Saigon* and *Buddy*, Clare's more than proved her capabilities.

Once during a visit to a Sandown Hilary Hall pantomime, you could sense the audience were mesmerised by one of the young babes. Somehow it seemed her life depended on that show, such was her enthusiasm and hard work. Just a year or two on, I was to write much about Seaview's Lucy Baker. Suddenly she was on-stage at the Chichester Festival Theatre with Keith Michelle and Jenny Seagrove. Talking about Jenny, the star of so many major television adaptations of Barbara Taylor-Bradford novels and numerous movies, we caught up with her in a play at the Kings, Southsea. That afternoon was rather special – in more ways than one. Heather and I were made a pot of tea by Jenny. Hayley Mills was also in the same company – and I interviewed them both.

By mutual agreement, Heather stayed out of the actual interviews – and always does. To be honest, to get the best out of a glamorous star you need a little harmless flirting from both parties to make an interview really work. That's never easy with your wife watching.

Wootton's Phyllida Crowley-Smith is another immense home-grown talent. How proud I felt when watching her in *Phantom of the Opera*, at Her Majesty's. In that West End dressing room her temperament was exactly the same as when sitting in her mother's lounge – except there were no hot flapjacks.

The mainland radio success of local Island presenters like Charlie Brook, Rick Jackson, James Hemming and Cameron Smith pleased me no end. I encouraged them as much as I could. There are others in the wings like Tom Stroud, Dominic Green, Duncan Smith and Gavin Harris. These days young Islanders seem to have more confidence in crossing the Solent to enhance their career prospects.

Watching many young local footballers playing in Premier and Football League soccer has been rewarding too. In my lifetime Wes Maughan went to Southampton and then Reading, Keith Allen went to Portsmouth, Grimsby, Luton, Stockport and Plymouth, Wayne Talkes also went to the Saints. Kieron Baker played 217 games for Bournemouth, Gareth Williams played for Aston Villa, under Graham Taylor, before moving on to Barnsley, Northampton, Scarborough and Hull; Gary Rowett regularly played in the Premiership for Derby and then joined Birmingham City, and Lee Bradbury, once of Cowes Sports, was a sensation at Portsmouth before moving on to Manchester City and Crystal Palace. Now Bournemouth's James Hayter seems to have a great future in the game. The Island can be proud of them all.

There are a few more who really should have made it. In the end, for various reasons, they didn't. Names like John Sothcott, Tony Grimwade, Barry Allen, Chris Cheverton, Mark Deacon and Simon Smith immediately spring to mind.

It was with more than a little trepidation in April, 1981, when I headed to the Sandown Pavilion to interview Pete Murray, who was then hosting a popular Radio 2 show, *Open House*. A week or two earlier Pete's son had tragically died. Our interview had been arranged many weeks earlier and I would have been quite content to forget the idea in view of his terrible family loss. That Pavilion live broadcast was his first public appearance since the death of his son.

Pete, one of the all-time great broadcasters of British radio, not forgetting Luxembourg, was keen to keep our date. There is always that self-doubt as to whether you should mention a recent bereavement of a close relative. Sometimes, of course, it can help. On this occasion the opportunity to place my hand on his shoulder and say I'd been thinking about him, was all that was needed. As to be expected, Pete Murray gave a very professional interview.

When requested, I always send copies of newspaper interviews or radio programmes to star names. Some are not interested at all. I sent a copy of the *Stage Talk* feature to Pete Murray at the BBC. One Sunday evening, shortly afterwards, we were sat at home watching television, when the 'phone rang. It was Pete Murray from Broadcasting House. If we would care to listen to his late night Radio 2 show, he would play a request for us – and he did. That was a marvellous way to say thank you.

Sean was beginning to show a real interest in coming on interviews, and when the invitation came for breakfast at the Sandringham Hotel, Sandown, with Jonathan King, who'd had a club gig the night before, he jumped at the opportunity to meet another star broadcaster. Jonathan also produced some amazing hit records and that cool television show, *Entertainment USA*.

Sean and fast-talking friend Jonathan King.

Mary O'Hara was the most fascinating lady. For many years, by her own choosing, she'd been restricted to life in a convent. The '60s had passed her by and she came out not even knowing who the Beatles were.

When Mary appeared at the Sandown Pavilion on May 11, 1982, she enjoyed a sell-out. At her request, our scheduled interview was postponed until the next day, as she had a headache.Then came the invitation for breakfast at the Winterbourne Hotel, Bonchurch, early the next morning.

When the time came for our taped interview, Mary suggested we walked around the garden in the early morning sunshine, sharing the microphone in the bracing Bonchurch air.

I remember when John Farrant, then the leisure director of South Wight Borough, told me that Tommy Cooper was coming for a short season at Sandown, in August '82 – I was so excited. Tommy, a true comedy genius, was one of the real great stars of British entertainment and the most impersonated name in show business.

I seldom missed a Tommy Cooper appearance. We got together early in the week for an interview and then he invited me down almost every night to join him in his dressing room. At that time he was unwell, suffering from leg trouble. The audiences would never have guessed. Tommy seemed lonely and was so glad of the company. We really hit it off. He also went to Shanklin to meet some old friends, Sy and Isa Lyn, Sid and Eve Edwards, from the Magic Box.

Tommy Cooper with Island friends Sy and Isa Lyn.

During our regular chats Tommy introduced me to a lady who had arrived, later in the week, to join him on the Island. He made a discreet point of telling me it wasn't his wife. That made no difference to me. I've still got a head full of showbiz secrets and have no interest in the private lives of stars. That should remain private. I kept his secret, as did everyone else in the business. I was disappointed, a few years after his sad death, when this lady friend sold her story to the press.

I'll never forget those late night conversations. I was just grateful to be invited into his company. Like millions of others I was watching *Live From The Palladium* the night Tommy died on stage. That would have been his chosen end, that's for sure. Some while after that tragic night, Jimmy Tarbuck and the show's writer, Wally Malston, both related their memories of that unforgettable evening. Poor Howard Keel had to sing just in front of Tommy, with only the curtain in between, whilst doctors tried to save his life.

There has always been a certain mystique surrounding Freddie Starr, who enjoys a reputation of being something of a wild character. What's he really like off stage? In 1982 I found out at the Sandown Pavilion where he'd been booked for his Isle of Wight début. There were stories that he wouldn't do

Freddie Starr – another Sandown Pavilion triumph.

interviews and was hard to deal with. In the '80s I just didn't have any problems at all. In this business it's who you know and how you've treated them.

Back in 1976 I'd met Leon Fisk, of the Dallas Boys, for the very first time. They were brilliant on all those old '50s and '60s TV shows like *Oh Boy!* We all instantly hit it off. Sadly all the original Dallas Boys have now retired. Joe Smith and Bob Wragg were the last to go, in the '80s.

Leon Fisk, who just loved teasing me, on or off-stage, had moved into management with his Mockingbird company and was looking after Freddie Starr. He promised me an interview and Fred did just that. I enjoyed the company of Freddie and his unpredictability. He was always so kind to me. Perhaps it was pity. On one occasion he even saw me despite having

real 'flu symptoms. He loved showing off, particularly if a young lady was in the dressing room. I took some stick from him. Since Freddie left Leon's management, I've not been so lucky.

Those stars who came in the '80s for summer seasons owed it all to Jimmy Tarbuck. Back in the '60s he first appeared in Sunday concerts at both the Sandown Pavilion and the Shanklin Theatre. On some occasions he would over-run at Sandown and would jest that if given the keys, he would lock up. One night, Don Moody threw on the keys. It brought the house down.

Tarby first came in 1979 to build on the success of Mike and Bernie Winters. He played to a 98% capacity over six weeks. Incredible figures and, suddenly, Sandown was up there against the big entertainment resorts of Blackpool, Bournemouth, Great Yarmouth and Scarborough. This was a new dimension for end-of-pier summer entertainment. Jimmy was at the height of his success and he wowed them every single night. More locals went than ever before.

Jimmy has always been one of my favourite comics and his topical material left the punters helpless with laughter. We had a mutual friend, in scriptwriter Wally Malston, and they were memorable times. The artists had fish and chip suppers on stage after the shows and what nights they were. Jim returned in '81 with what was probably the best summer show ever seen on the Isle of Wight. It starred JT, Kenny Lynch, Aiden J. Harvey, Denise Nolan, Pan's People and the Johnny Wiltshire Orchestra.

Whenever I went into Tarby's dressing room I was on my guard. He was a great television fan and if he was in the middle of watching something, I just sat down and said nothing. He appreciated that.

I found an old Kenny Lynch *Music For Pleasure* LP and took it down to be signed – as well as to create a few laughs. When Tarby saw it and read the gushing sleeve notes, the backstage was in uproar. He read it all out loud and added some of his own thoughts. We think Kenny was even blushing – but couldn't tell. Jimmy Tarbuck came back in 1989, the year of the Pavilion fire. Heather and I had met him on our Palladium silver wedding trip, in '88, and Tarby dropped the hint that he'd like a return to Sandown. I whispered in a few ears. They must have been the right ones.

Jimmy Tarbuck, pictured with theatre manager Jan Fletcher and 'Lynchy', brought a new era to the Sandown Pavilion.

CHAPTER EIGHT

CILLA, JEREMY & MISS RICE-DAVIES

WHO COULD follow Jimmy Tarbuck into the Sandown Pavilion? Cilla Black certainly could and she summered here in 1983, on the recommendation of her Liverpool pal. Like JT, Ted Rogers, Frankie Howerd and others, Cilla stayed in a secluded Ventnor country house. Cilla loved early morning gossips with her cleaner, Gloria.

Weekly Post and *The News* reporter Richard Wright was asked to do an interview with Cilla, for the Portsmouth paper. It was not easy. I'd already been trying for a week or two to break the ice. In the end I got the thumbs up from husband Bobby. Richard Wright was delighted when I offered to do his feature for *The News*.

Cilla Black had fascinated both locals and holidaymakers all summer. Every night hundreds waited outside just to see her walk into the theatre. That's real stardom for you.

During our conversation she revealed she'd just been offered a contract to make a television comeback, with a different type of show. That was the start of *Surprise, Surprise* and *Blind Date,* and other shows like that. A long way from *Anyone Who Had A Heart.*

I must admit to having been extremely nervous on the interview night. In the end, I needn't have worried. On her closing night on the Island she paid me a real compliment. Thanks Cilla.

There were some epic Sandown seasons in the '80s. Norman Wisdom came and so did that supreme professional, Bob Monkhouse. Who can forget the late Billy Dainty? Nights with him were action-packed. He had incredible energy on and off stage. Little and Large were another act who brought out the crowds.

Earlier on I revealed how I'd had a problem recording an interview with Felix Bowness, due to a human error. Mine! Thankfully, that's only ever happened on one other occasion – and I have a good excuse.

When you sit very close to Julie Rogers it really is hard to concentrate on anything, particularly to do with a tape recorder. Perhaps I'd also remembered she liked older men. On the way home we put the tape in the car player and there was silence – at least until I'd realised what had happened. This was to be the nucleus of a *Weekly Post* feature. With my wife taking notes I remembered most of the interview, from barely fifteen minutes earlier. No-one ever knew. Since then I've interviewed Julie on several more occasions – and remembered to push in the red button.

I did have another scare many years later with Paul Daniels. The interview was only confirmed by mobile 'phone on the Fishbourne car ferry. The venue was to be Hayling Island, at one of the Warner centres. My first port of call was the Chichester Festival Theatre, where I met Bob Grant from *On The Buses.*

I arrived at Paul's chalet and was a little daunted at the prospect. I knew I would have to work hard to get the best out of him. This mission was duly accomplished and Paul quickly warmed to the conversation. As I dismantled my radio recording equipment, I noticed Paul's microphone was switched off.

Then came that feeling of blind panic. I knew he wouldn't have the time to do another stint. Sean came with me and on the way back to the car I explained my anguish. Once in the car I switched on the DAT recorder and all was well.

To this day, I still believe Paul Daniels' sleight of hand technique had somehow turned off that mike, at the end of the conversation. I've seen him twice, since then, and have not been brave enough to ask him.

A year or two later, at Warner's Bembridge, I interviewed his lovely wife Debbie McGee – and her old man left us to it. What a lovely lady, too.

Successful Islanders have long been an inspiration for me. Early on in my journalistic career I set a target of tracking down as many as I possibly could. Some took longer than others to trace.

Brian Murphy, born in Ventnor, was one of the first. I recall that he remembered the Island's steam trains with particular affection. I travelled to the Pier Theatre, Bournemouth, where I was to meet up with Brian. Millions remember him from *George and Mildred*. I also met him again years later in Southsea. In more recent times Brian's been seen as the 'victim' on *This Is Your Life*, and he was also the only good thing in that awful television series *Mrs Merton and Malcolm*.

Sheila Hancock, actually born at Blackgang, had heard rumours of more recent happenings in the area, but not on cold days. Mind you, some of those naturalists think nothing of it. Our rendez-vous point was the foyer of the BBC's Broadcasting House. Eventually Sheila emerged from the lift, with a worried expression. "There is a change of plan. A taxi is due to pick me up in five minutes to take me to the station. I've now got to go to Derby," exclaimed Sheila.

Somehow we managed enough conversation in those five minutes to fill a *Stage Talk* column.

One of the most famous Islanders of all time is Jeremy Irons. The Hollywood superstar went to Ryde's Little Appley School and still remembers the family house in St Helens. Jeremy was actually born in a Cowes nursing home and then rushed to St Helens. He's still very pro 'Goose Island' and told me: "We lived overlooking St Helens Harbour, which is what Bembridge people think is Bembridge Harbour."

Jeremy's was the first voice ever heard on Isle of Wight Radio. His recorded message officially launched the station at Easter, 1990. His father, Paul, was once the company secretary of Saunders-Roe and his name, P. J. Irons, was on all the company's transport fleet.

When I walked into the dressing room of Stratford's Royal Shakespeare Theatre and saw Jeremy Irons sat there, it was a proud moment for me. It was all that I expected – and more. Stars of his magnitude are rather special – and you can feel that. Ever the gentleman, he had originally suggested we did the interview over the 'phone, to save a trip to Stratford. To me that's never been an option. So many journalists and radio presenters claim to have met their star guests face to face. In more cases than you might care to imagine, this is not so.

For me, the thrill of being in the company of the person is as important as the interview itself. You certainly get an instant inspiration and, most definitely, a more genuine impression of the person you are interviewing. The vibes just take over.

Jeremy Irons – from St Helens to Holly-wood. He's proud to be an Islander. I turned down a telephone interview to meet him in person.

(Still from 'Reversal of Fortune' courtesy of Sovereign Pictures.)

So often, too, things can happen, in a live in-person situation, that are lost over 'phone and studio-to-studio lines. There have also been stories of impostors being at the end of telephone lines. Impressionists can be quite convincing. On one famous occasion a cocky young mainland presenter thought he had Sean Connery in a station link-up. It wasn't such a scoop a few days later, when an impressionist revealed it was not Mr Connery at all.

In '90s radio there are now so many interviews that are tagged 'down the line'. This means a guest can be in a studio in London or Scotland talking to a presenter in any other radio station in Britain. The quality is so good you can actually believe they are sitting together. You can easily spot the difference though, if you listen closely. Is this cheating? You'll have to make up your own mind.

Back in the '70s I had a 'phone call from a guy in East Cowes telling me he was the ex-Shadows drummer Tony Meehan and how much would I pay him for an interview? I did remind him that I had never ever paid for an interview. We made a date to meet at the British Hovercraft Club, where he drank.

I had compiled a lot of searching questions that could only have been answered by the real Tony Meehan. The only problem was, this other guy didn't even turn up. Unbeknown to him, I had already taken a good look through the club windows, a night or two earlier, and it certainly wasn't the hit recorder of *Diamonds* and *Scarlett O'Hara*.

Cowes-born Cliff Michelmore had always proved an elusive Islander. My mother-in-law had been in the same school class as him. The first time I ever saw him, in person, was at the inaugural County Cricket match at the J. S. Whites sports ground, Cowes, when Hampshire played Worcestershire. His lovely wife, Jean Metcalfe, was with him.

43

The day we got married, October 12, 1963, Cliff and his wife were also at the end of Ryde Pier, as we set sail on our honeymoon. They were giving two other newly weds, John Michelmore, a local relative, and his wife, a family honeymoon send-off.

When the *Post* came on stream in 1975, I wrote to Cliff to see if I could do an interview with him. At that time it was not convenient. For several more years I continued my pursuit, with no success at all. Finally I had a real break-through, in 1998, and was invited to Cliff and Jean's gorgeous cottage in the Hampshire countryside. It was all down to another local relative of Cliff's, June Butcher. We go back a long way.

Cliff Michelmore was the consummate professional. Despite praying for a smooth operation, I had a slight technical problem with a microphone lead. It meant a false start. Why does it happen when you're interviewing an inter-viewer? Then I called him Cliff Richard. Perhaps it wasn't going to be my day.

When the great man proved to be just as human, by completely tying up an answer to a question, I felt a lot better. We had to do that bit again. He was such a fascinating subject and during the '70s was the most televised face in Britain. He even loaned me his own CDs to play on the programme.

Another long distance chase came in the hunt for Ian Bannen, whose family lived in Ventnor for many years. Ian, who has made many top movies like *Flight Of The Phoenix*, *The Hill*, *Station Six Sahara* and *Waking Ned*, has always been a regular visitor to the Island. His charming wife, Marilyn, had initially replied to my first letter, from America, where Ian was making yet another movie. For the next few years his hectic schedule prevented any hope of a meeting.

That original request was for the Isle of Wight Hospital Radio and the *Weekly Post*. When we eventually got together the Island tabloid was extinct. To keep my word, the interview was also played on the local hospital radio network, as well as Isle of Wight Radio. Ian has a great sense of fun and I loved the interview. How did I finally catch him? Probably my tenacity in never giving up the chase and the fact that Heather saw him in a local swimming pool and made herself known. Did I ever pay her that commission?

During 1983 I had a 'phone call from Billy Padley, who was still at Radio Victory. One of their sales promotion girls had actually cut her first record. Could he bring her over to the Vine Inn, St Helens, for a chat? I subsequently managed to get features on her in the *Weekly Post* and *The Stage*, the latter being her first-ever national publicity.

The young lady who came to the Vine was then named Jules. Five years later Bill sent me a pre-release copy of a superlative new album, co-produced by him, featuring an exciting new singer – Julia Fordham. It was the same girl. Julia went on to enjoy eight chart hits, between 1988 and '94.

I love watching cabaret acts and on so many occasions holiday centre managers, agents and punters have tipped me off about entertainers working the Island circuit. Several have gone on to achieve lasting fame.

In the summer of '84 Rose-Marie had just released her début album and was touring the Island Warner centres, as the mid-week cabaret attraction. Punters loved her powerful vocals, rich Irish brogue and great stories.

She had other prize assets, too. We saw quite a lot of each other. One night I saw more than I bargained for. I knocked on her dressing room door and walked straight in. I closed my eyes and guided myself out. I was definitely more embarrassed than Rose.

Since those humble beginnings on the Island, Rose has sold millions of albums and enjoyed sell-out theatre tours. I still look forward to her great welcoming hug, when we meet up. It keeps an old man very happy.

I was invited to Warner's Bembridge, to watch a young comedy star, who had originally been one of the company's green coats. The name was Joe Pasquale. What an ace nut case! His act was quite sensational and I gave him a rave review in *The Stage*. He also had a rather strange high-pitched voice. Within a couple of years he was on the *Royal Variety Show*.

Joe's quite a character and my daughter never believed his voice was really that squeaky. We put it to the test. I had to 'phone Joe at his home to arrange an interview to celebrate his sudden stardom. He was due to come back to the Island for a star cabaret week-end at Harcourt Sands. Caroline listened on the upstairs extension and quickly realised he also talked like that at home.

During one of his star nights at Harcourt, he slipped away to the nearby Nodes Point Holiday Centre to see an old showbiz pal. Joe, being Joe, volunteered to read out the bingo numbers, in some sort of disguise. It didn't work too well because his voice was the same. The St Helens holidaymakers were never quite sure if it really was Joe. He was wearing a baseball cap and glasses and was introduced as Billy Milly and his Amazing Dancing Chickweed.

Tony Scott, whose late father Bill Scott-Gordon put on many successful summer season shows at Sandown, during the '50s and '60s, is one of those stand-up comedians who has the timing and experience to slip into acting. He appeared in a snooker movie and toured Britain in a farce called *A Bedfull of Foreigners*.

Tony rang me the week before their Southsea booking to ask if I was interested in interviewing Mandy Rice-Davies. What a silly question! Having just been out of my teens at the time of the Profumo Scandal, I knew a good blonde when I saw one. In her case – she wasn't quite so good, if you know what I mean.

I remember the day well. It was my birthday. Tony's lovely wife Jenny was also celebrating hers and had made a special cake for both of us. We shared it with Mandy, Tony, Heather and another star from the show, Don Maclean.

We saw a matinée performance and, suddenly, in between shows, there I was locked in a room with Mandy Rice-Davies – and that was work? What a stunning lady! Mr Profumo and his friends certainly had good taste and this was twenty years on.

After the interview I joined the rest of the cast, plus Heather, in the nearby

A back-stage birthday treat – with Tony and Jenny Scott, Don Maclean and Mandy Rice-Davies.

transport café. Mandy arrived a few minutes later and there was only one seat left, next to a lorry driver. He, clearly, had no idea who she was. I've often wondered what that guy would have made of it. If someone had said to him, twenty years earlier, that he would one day share a table with Mandy Rice-Davies, he would needed to have believed in miracles.

Mandy had enjoyed a varied life since those days in the '60s when she left London in rather a hurry. She'd been a dancer, singer, actress and author – and been through a few husbands too. I just loved her company and personality. I might not have coped twenty years earlier, being a young and naïve Isle of Wight boy.

A few weeks after our interview Mandy sent me a super hand-written letter. In her teens Mandy's idols were Albert Schweitzer, Colonel Harry Llewellyn, Winston Churchill and Clark Gable. It's a funny old world. Her dream was to be a missionary. "In the end I became Mandy Rice-Davies," she teased, in her most seductive voice.

There were some other palpitating moments in that same year. In the autumn the Isle of Wight Song Festival was held at Westridge. It was extremely well organised by Stephen Gold and sponsored by Wightlink. There were stars in abundance, too. I've thought of four of the ladies many times in the past fourteen years or so – and three were in the same pop group.

Some close friends will know how special it was for me to interview the Three Degrees, who starred in a special concert in the marquee. There was a press conference to meet the girls and the local media was well represented. There was Mike Merritt, from the *Echo*, a pleasant young guy from the *County Press*, who knew nothing about the girls, and yours truly.

Mike did all the talking – which was not unexpected. He wanted to talk about Prince Charles and the Three Degrees, even though that had been over-played for so many years. I sensed the girls felt the same way. The *County Press* guy just listened.

When it was all over the girls were concerned that I had also said nothing. I then asked if I could do something different and not talk about Prince Charles, as the other press guys had left. So for fifteen minutes I was surrounded by the Three Degrees – and didn't blush. Things had changed for the better. In the Test Match radio commentaries they always have a champagne moment. This would qualify for one of mine.

These three sent my degrees soaring.

What a few days that was! American singer-songwriter Gerard Kenny, who has since become a good friend, gave a sensational show. His own songs include *I Made It Through The Rain*, also recorded by Barry Manilow, *Fantasy*, *I Could Be So Good For You*, which is the *Minder* theme, and *New York, New York*.

Another guest for the *Stage Talk* column was Geoff Stephens, the phenomenal songwriter, whose hits include *The Crying Game*. Also at Westridge was Sonny Curtis, who had been in Buddy Holly's original backing band. A year or two later, at Harcourt Sands, I met two more of Buddy's original Crickets, Jerry Allison and Joe Mauldin.

Peter Powell, Jan Francis and Gerard Kenny at the 1984 Isle of Wight Song Contest.

Another most welcome guest was top Radio 1 presenter Peter Powell. I managed quite a scoop from Peter. At that time his national radio career seemed invincible and he was the inspiration for many other aspiring young jocks. In our conversation he exclusively revealed that he was aiming to pull out of radio and go into a another aspect of the business. Now he's become a top manager and agent. A few days after the *Weekly Post* interview a piece appeared in the *Sun*. You never know who reads a small local newspaper. There are one or two notable 'stringers' who pass local stories on to the national media, for much reward. Good luck to them.

Also at that one and only Isle of Wight Song Festival was Jan Francis, one of the stars of that marvellous television series *Just Good Friends*. Jan had been a regular visitor here for years, having close friends on the Island. With Vince (Paul Nicholas) nowhere in sight, we had a nice quiet chat and a cup of coffee. Jan is another talented actress who is so charming and modest, off-stage.

The Shadows were responsible for many youngsters taking up the guitar. Hank Marvin was one of the genuine British pop heroes, particularly with the young lads, many of whom wanted to look and sound like their idol. In August '84 the Shadows were booked for the Sandown Pavilion and in no time at all the show was sold out. Several weeks earlier I'd written to the band's management requesting an interview. There was no reply but, being a born optimist, I remained hopeful.

My initial enquiry to the road manager was met with the response that no-one had ever seen the letter. Unbeknown to him, something he said in our conversation confirmed it had been received. There was not a happy ending. Their manager would not allow them to be interviewed, despite enough time being available. I had a few albums to sign and they willingly did all that and chatted but were not allowed to be interviewed. Both Bruce Welch and Brian Bennett did apologise.

My good friend Jeff Stevenson, another youngster for whom I'd predicted a great future for, having first watched him as a seventeen-year-old at the Albany Prison Officers' Club, was the compère of the show but not even he could arrange it. Hank also signed some albums, with Jeff's persuasion, but would not let me go in and say a quick hello. I was more than a little aggrieved as I had promoted the show so much. I never bare grudges and am still a great admirer of the Shadows.

Lyn Paul, the beautiful blonde singer from the New Seekers, gave me one of the roughest rides ever during an interview. It was in 1986 at Sandown and Lyn was supporting Cannon and Ball, along with the marvellous Jessica Martin. I'd successfully interviewed Jessica and Tom and Bobby and was hoping for an equally productive third interview.

For a while I wondered just why I'd made the effort to interview Lyn. Homework, as already mentioned, is the key to obtaining satisfactory interviews. In a pop reference book the text clearly stated Lyn Paul was born in Australia. When I opened our taped conversation I asked how an Australian girl had ended up in the New Seekers. I knew the original Seekers, a different group entirely, had been Australian. I'd hardly finished the question when Lyn asked me to stop the tape because I was hopelessly wrong. On the resumption it was not plain sailing either. Every point seemed to be questioned by her.

This was a new experience for me and I was both embarrassed and angry. I went home for an hour or two, before the show, and looked into that reference book. Armed with the book I went back to her dressing room and showed her the Australian story and other facts. She instantly apologised and the matter was closed. In my *Weekly Post* feature I revealed the story and, discreetly, took a gentle knock at Miss Paul. On-stage she was brilliant and I raved about her performance.

I decided to send her a copy of the article and back came a wonderful letter, with more apologies. There was also an invitation to join her for a drink the next time she came to the Island. I really appreciated that.

Television soaps have never made much of an impression on me. I've never followed any of them and the only time I watch is if I'm due to meet someone from one of the shows. Then I need to become aware of a particular character. Some find it hard to believe that I've never seen a complete episode of *Coronation Street* or *EastEnders*. My daughter can always help out on advice for interviews. She's quite a fan of at least half a dozen soaps. The six-part drama series are much more to my liking. I prefer to see a start and finish to a story line, within a few episodes. Being extremely pro-British, I have no interest in American soaps, dramas or comedy shows.

In the past twenty years I've been impressed by the attitudes and friendliness of many of the soap stars that I've met. My roadie on most occasions is my daughter Caroline. She knows all about them and has even shared a meal with one or two.

A few years ago I'd interviewed Ian Smith, who plays Harold Bishop in *Neighbours*, and sent him a copy of the radio interview. He 'phoned my home to thank me and was pleased with the segment. Caroline answered the 'phone and was highly impressed. Some of her friends were quite envious.

Others that spring to mind include Les Hill, Bruce Samazan, Ian Kelsey, Ray Meagher and Nicola Stapleton. With soap stars, just under half the population know who they are. To the remainder, they are completely unknown. It's a strange situation.

Meeting Chris Quinten at Bogey's – the Sandown nightclub – back in 1986, was an eventful night. He played Brian Tilsley in *Coronation Street*. Chris duly arrived, very late, and with a well-known local young lady. That was none of my business. I turned a blind eye and he gave me a great interview. Others I enjoyed meeting at Bogey's have included Janice Long, Limahl, George McCrae, Gina G, Bruno Brookes, Edwin Starr and Hazell Dean.

I did turn down the chance of interviewing an unknown pop group a few years ago. Wayne Peak gave me the opportunity but I never followed it through. They were here to record a video. Take That went on to become massive. You can't win them all.

In the '80s I was a regular at Colonel Bogey's, as an interviewer. The bouncers were brilliant and really made a fuss of me. They were always very helpful and never failed to produce a chair, cup of tea and a rich tea biscuit. Were they trying to tell me something?

During my life I've been lucky to have met many famous people. To me this has always been an honour and privilege. I love show business and its people, which compensates for so many unsocial hours.

Particularly in my *Weekly Post* days, meeting Page 3 girls always created quite a stir. It was never difficult to tempt a photographer to come with you. Chris Thwaites seemed to get the luck of the draw – one of the perks of being chief photographer. Another superb *Post* photographer was Murray Sanders, who's now working for the *Daily Mail*.

When Linda Lusardi was appearing at a local nightclub she stayed at the Cliff Tops hotel. I was allowed to go to her room and took along Chris, as well. As soon as she saw the camera there was a little problem. Linda was off duty and not really dressed for a local paper shot. It was all resolved in the end and she is such a super lady. At that time, her boyfriend, later her husband, was a Kevin Keegan look-a-like. I had quite a shock when I entered her room and found him sat up in bed. They were both perfect hosts – and he did get teased.

A few months earlier Sam Fox had made a public appearance at Westridge

'Touch Me' was Sam Fox's first hit record. Many at Westridge felt the same way.

and thousands turned up – including Messrs Hannam and Thwaites. Once again, Chris turned down a flower show to join me. More to look at, I suppose.

There was a hot-air balloon at the event and it should have remained tethered to the ground. With Sam Fox aboard, surprisingly, it suddenly took off and disappeared over several fields, which worried her bodyguards, who were still on the ground, as well as the organisers. Eventually she was rescued and came back to wow the punters.

Martin Rockley, who worked at the centre and was an old football mate of mine, promised an interview with Miss Fox. He could arrange it – and he did. What a lady! Whatever her minder wanted, I went along with. Then Sam issued me a challenge: "Punch him in the stomach as hard as you can." It had no effect at all – well, only to my hand.

True to form, after the interview was published came the questions. This time, not the usual ones. More a case of "What were they like?" I could honestly lie and say, I never even looked.

CHAPTER NINE

A BOUQUET FROM PARKY
& A PURR FROM EARTHA

ALL JOURNALISTS, broadcasters, critics and performers alike have a god. With me, it was most definitely Michael Parkinson. That view has never changed. Like so many, I was brought up on Parky's shows, when the guests were world superstars. Where have they all gone these days?

Michael was due on the Island to star in a Sunday concert at Sandown. I was terrified on my way to the interview with him. This man was the *crème de la crème* and I was just a local paper showbiz columnist. This really was a dream come true. It turned out to be a day to remember.

He was a marvellous host and nothing was too much trouble. We chatted about showbiz, sport and just about everything. Then came one of the greatest moments in my life.

We were talking about interviews and techniques. Suddenly Parky made a comment which made the hairs on my head (there were many in those days) virtually stand up. He said: "You're a good interviewer. You obviously like people, you listen, show interest and do your homework." Thank you Michael Parkinson.

There was an after-show dressing room invitation for Heather and me. Michael had never forgotten he was a young reporter on a Barnsley newspaper. I'm so glad his chat shows were brought back in 1998. Seeing him hosting *Give Us A Clue* was such an insult to his talents.

Another media hero of mine was Ray Moore. What a superb broadcaster and in a class of his own. So much talent, and yet so much modesty and humility as well. That's a real broadcaster.

Ray came for a Cowes Week Radio 2 live broadcast and we met at Newport's Bugle Hotel. He had only just woken up and instantly apologised for keeping me waiting. My young daughter Caroline came with me and we were both absorbed by his special brand of hospitality.

Having subsequently read his wife's book, he must have known he was unwell at the time he came to the Island. His death, from cancer, was such a tragedy.

I can remember teasing him about those hit records he made like *O' My Father Had A Rabbit*. Ray was not an egotistical broadcaster. I've met a few who are – and none are as good as he was. Ray was genuinely interested in the interviewer and their way of life and family interests.

I look on 1987 as a vintage year. When Peter Skellern came to Sandown I was sent the usual biog, picture and show details. I could hardly believe my eyes. In his backing band was a guitarist named Vic Flick. Vic who? To many guitar fans this man was a real mentor. Vic had made his name in the John Barry Seven, twanging his way on huge hits like *Hit and Miss* and, wait for it,

The James Bond Theme. Vic Flick had played the most famous guitar riffs in the world in all the Bond movies.

Amazingly, he was flattered when approached for an interview. Years later I wrote to him inviting him on to my radio show. He would have come – but was living in America. One of his greatest pleasures was sailing his boat to the Island – unbeknown to any of us.

During that summer several of the *Copy Cats* television show came to Sandown for a one-nighter and I knew virtually all of them. It was a wonderful line-up including Mike Osman, Allan Stewart, Mark Walker, Hilary O'Neil, Aiden J. Harvey and Andrew O'Connor. Interviewing them was a trifle manic but hugely enjoyable. I'd quickly found out many

Vic Flick – the most famous guitar riffs in the world.

years earlier that you need to have a great sense of humour, particularly mixing with comedians. The times I've been teased and set-up are endless and this lot were no exception.

I had an unexpected bonus, too. The sum of £250. That was the fee for over six months *Stage Talks* in one hit. The *TV Times* rang up my wife and asked if I could write an article on the Copy Cats, by Monday. This was Friday lunchtime. Apparently, I was the only journalist in Britain who had interviewed them all together. The copy was sent on time.

Imagine my excitement at opening the *TV Times*, dated 31 October to 6 November, 1987, to see my very own two-page feature. There it was in millions of homes – written by John Hammon! They had misspelt my name.

Derek Hunt's country music nights were always something special at Pagham Place. The straw bales, makeshift bar and country music were an unbeatable combination. Derek's reputation attracted some of Britain's top country acts, including the Cotton Mill Boys, Leapy Lee, who revealed he'd been to the Island before but was then wearing Little Arrows instead of singing about them, Patsy Powell and, from the USA, Wesley Parker.

Among the homegrown favourites was Shag Connors and the Carrot Crunchers. A few years earlier they had been particularly popular at the Ponda Rosa. On this occasion Shag, who brought a huge cockerel on stage, was clearly unwell. His cheery nature was uncannily subdued. We did have a chat but Shag was not himself. Sadly, that was to be his last interview. The west country gem only played a couple more gigs. He died a few days later.

Mike (Shag) Connors was also a most under-rated songwriter. One of his greatest compositions was a song called *The Cotswolds*. The band is still going with his son, Mart, at the helm.

Anthony Bishop had worked on the Island for John Redgrave and was always most helpful in working with the media. At the tail end of '87 Des O'Connor made a long-awaited comeback to the Sandown Pavilion. It was his first visit since the early '60s. Des brought his one-man show and it proved a complete sell-out.

Des, who has such a superb television chat show, seldom does interviews himself. On this occasion his London press office had stated he wouldn't be doing any on the Isle of Wight. I arrived at the band call, just in case, and ran straight into Anthony. After our initial greeting, he told me he was now Des's personal assistant. I reminded him he owed me a favour or two, from past press publicity for his shows.

At that precise time Des was away from the Pavilion but would be back quite soon. An hour or so later Anthony rang me at home to say Des would now see me, after the show. What a bonus that was – thirty hilarious minutes in the company of Des O'Connor. On-stage Des rewarded his audience with a quite brilliant show. I've tried since on several occasions to get a reprise interview, with not a hint of luck.

As a schoolboy, I'd written to Eartha Kitt and received back from her a stunning signed photo. Yes, I was a confirmed fan. My loyalty to Eartha Kitt had not escaped the attention of the *Post's* founding editor Keith Newbery, to whom I owe a great deal. He always showed great confidence in me and was a constant source of encouragement.

I once committed an unforgivable sin in the eyes of Keith Newbery. I actually 'phoned him during an episode of *Coronation Street*. I thought he'd forgiven me, until one particular night. Eartha Kitt, looking sensational, was being interviewed in an early evening TV chat show. My 'phone rang and I had to drag myself away. It was Mr Newbery getting his own back.

When Eartha was in the West End starring in *Follies*, in a whim of excited anticipation I wrote to her, asking if I could come up to London for an interview. I had nothing to lose. Then my worries really began – she agreed.

I'd briefly met Eartha, once before, backstage at the Kings, Southsea, purely to sign a few albums. Never before in my life had I seen such a beautiful woman. Now, more than a few years on, I was off to the big city to really meet her. Once again I was hit by pre-interview nerves. En route to the ferry I called into Haylands Farm to buy her a local plant, and took some Terry's chocolate. This was not the occasion to take chances. I knew her fancies – well, some of them.

After a nervous wait, I was invited into Miss Kitt's tiny dressing room in the Shaftesbury Theatre. Eartha was sat working on her crochet and didn't even look up. By her tone of voice I knew she was impatient to start the interview. I took a deep breath and began.

Then Eartha put down the crochet.

There was no doubt I was feeling the strain. The chance to meet one of my schoolboy infatuations was hardly going to plan – and the plant and chocolates were still outside the dressing room door. Had that been my first big mistake?

After five heart-pumping minutes my morale suddenly took a turn for the better. Eartha put down her crochet work and concentrated on our conversation. Then she started to purr – and so did I. As long as Keith Newbery didn't walk in, I was up and running. We were enjoying each others company – and the plant and chocolates were still up my sleeve, if you know what I mean.

I almost glided back to the underground station. The ultimate outcome was all that I could have hoped for. But, there was more to come. After reading the article, Eartha sent me a handwritten letter of appreciation. She also suggested that if I was ever anywhere near a theatre where she was appearing, I was to make myself known.

That was put to the test a few months later on a Mother's Day, in Southsea, on Eartha's return to the Kings. Within two minutes of presenting the letter at the stage door, I was in her dressing room and so were Heather and Caroline. By then, Eartha was well over sixty and looked a little different to her screen and stage image. This time, she actually let my daughter finish off her Mother's Day chocolates.

An hour later, when she ran on to that Southsea stage, the transformation was better than anyone on *Stars In Their Eyes*. There was the sex appeal, glamour, shimmering dress and that unbelievable purring voice. Cat Woman was in her element. My daughter just couldn't believe it.

The chance to go on location doesn't come that often. Thanks to Alison Pope, then a junior press officer at TVS, who now has a more senior post with Meridian, I was invited to spend a Valentine's Day with the cast of a Ruth Rendell television mystery, at Kings Markham, or Romsey to be precise. I had not missed any of the TV series that starred George Baker and Christopher Ravenscroft. It was a memorable day. I was picked up from the ferry and spent the whole day on the set with the actors and film crew, with lunch provided in the caravan. George was particularly good company and the whole cast were most welcoming. During a break from filming I noticed the Hampshire and England cricketer Robin Smith pedal by on an old bike. There is a lovely local

Robin Smith story. When he stayed overnight on the Island for a testimonial game, he was put up at the Lake home of Ryde cricketer Dave Tolfrey. Dave's young daughter, a keen Robin Smith fan, took in his early morning tea and saw this handsome muscled cricket ace sat up in bed. "I expect you could eat three Shredded Wheat," she nervously enquired. At that time there was a publicity campaign saying that only Ian Botham could eat more than two. Robin's now been a guest on my radio show on several occasions.

There was a 1990 Isle of Wight Pop Festival at Smallbrook Stadium, to mark the twentieth anniversary of the great Afton Down event. Boy George was headlining. He arrived late and unfortunately the crowds were disappointing. For a while there were stories circulating that he might not appear, which proved false. There was no time for a press conference but the rumours suggested he was at the Seaview Hotel.

The next morning I turned up, in hope, and George willingly obliged. It was quite a family affair, with Sean and Caroline joining us for a front garden coffee. Being Seaview, no-one worried Boy George at all. They are blasé at seeing famous people.

I went to both the Wootton and Freshwater Pop Festivals and enjoyed the atmosphere very much. There was no real trouble either. What great PR for the Island they were. We were the main news story on television news bulletins around the world. The small shops had a field day, which was much deserved.

Ronnie Hilton and Christine Westoll trusted me with their touching love story.

I'd always rated Ronnie Hilton one of the great British '50s crooners and when he came to the Island for a summer season, I got to know him and his wife Chrissie very well. One afternoon I was invited for afternoon tea at their rented Haylands bungalow. They had a unique story to tell and wanted to take me into their confidence.

Basically, the story was of an affair they'd had, in the '60s, when Christine Westoll was a dancer in an Oxford pantomime. Ronnie only went there to see two old showbiz pals. His own Christmas show had ended. He fell instantly in love with this seventeen-year-old dancer. Probably because he was told he had no chance with her, he tried even harder. There had been a lovechild from that relationship. In the end Ronnie made the decision to stay with his wife. The lovers did not meet again for another twenty years.

Their son, Simon, born in December 1966, wanted both mum and dad at his twenty-first birthday. Ronnie and Christine met up again. During those twenty years Ronnie had lost his lovely wife Joan. She had known about the affair but was prepared to fight for their marriage and had succeeded. Ronnie was also true to his word.

Following the tragic death of Joan, from cancer, Ronnie was at a low ebb. When he and Christine met again their romance blossomed and they are still together. Over Christmas 1998 a television dramatisation of their story was screened on ITV. During our Haylands conversation, back in '88, no-one knew of their story. They wanted me to write it but told me to do nothing until they had 'phoned me. The call did come very late that year. They were in quite a state. The *News of the World* had somehow unearthed the details and they were terrified it would be revealed as a tacky story, full of lust, passion and sex. It hadn't been that at all.

Within ten minutes of Ronnie's call I was talking to the *Daily Mail*. I explained the situation and they were keen to have an exclusive. My story was 'phoned to their copy-taker and the wheels were in motion. It was rewritten, obviously, to suit the *Mail's* style but it was handled very tastefully. We had won the race, too. The *News of the World* never did publish the story.

I've mentioned meeting Page 3 girls in hotel bedrooms but it's not always been that glamorous. When Peter Brennen booked Bernard Manning for his Island début, an interview had been pre-arranged. When I arrived at Puckpool, Bernard had just been driven in from Manchester. That made no difference, he was up for the interview.

When I knocked on the chalet door there was Bernard in his vest and underpants. I must admit, sitting on a bed with Bernard Manning wasn't one of the greatest moments of my life. Away from that mouthy stage persona, he's quite a kind and gentle man. I wouldn't want to upset him, though.

A few years later I actually had three men sat on a bed in the Melville Hall, Sandown – and they went on to be worth at least £30 million – even more than Big Bernard. This golden trio were Alan Shearer, Tim Flowers and Neil Ruddock. At that time they were all Southampton footballers, over for the dinner of the Island Saints' supporters.

Mike Reid has lived an eventful life. There have been obvious milestones like *The Comedians* and playing Frank Butcher in *EastEnders*. In between, he's endured several family tragedies and personal problems. Mike, by nature, is a born fighter. I've always enjoyed his company, as a friend and journalist. On one occasion he came to the Island during some unwelcome national publicity. He dismissed the minders and talked to me.

Matt Monro was beyond doubt Britain's greatest-ever singing stylist. His voice was in the class of American superstars like Sinatra, Tony Bennett and

Vic Damone. I'd first seen Matt at the Commodore Cinema, Ryde, on August 2, 1964, in a concert with the Pretty Things. What a bizarre combination that was. During his act Matt changed the lyric of his Eurovision song to "I love the Pretty Things". During the show the curtain was pulled down on the Pretty Things.

Matt came back for numerous appearances at the Sandown Pavilion, all with great success. Frank Sinatra was among his greatest fans. Their ilk will never be seen or appreciated again.

The last time I met Matt Monro was at the Savoy Country Club, Yarmouth,

The ultimate voice – Matt Monro.

when he came to sing to help raise funds for the RNLI. Having got to know him as a good mate, I went to his dressing room for a pre-show chat. Matt looked fit and bronzed, although thinner than we'd come to expect. I can remember remarking how healthy he looked. Matt replied with something like "Looks don't mean everything". I never gave it a second thought.

Just before the show I was in the gentlemen's toilet when an arrogant mainland yuppy came in and intoxicatingly uttered: "Matt Monro – I thought he was dead!" I shall never know how I didn't push him into the urinals. In hindsight, I wish I had. That night, as ever, Matt was in sparkling form.

It was only a month or two later when we heard an early morning Radio 2 news story that Matt was suffering from cancer. Such a loss to music and a really lovely man.

In 1998 Heather and I went to Matt's home in Harrow to renew our friendship with his widow Mickie. There were so many touching mementos of the great singer all around the house.

Matt's daughter Michelle arrived in mid-afternoon, having picked up her son Max from school. He wanted to sing on my tape recorder after I interviewed his nan. Max kept singing his favourite songs from *Oliver*. When it came to his turn on the microphone, he dried up completely and just wouldn't do it. It would have been such a gem. I have so many records of Matt and one by him and his son, Matt junior. That would have been the third generation Monro. Matt's surname is always spelt incorrectly. He once told me the easiest way to remember it. "It's an anagram of moron," quipped Matt.

Another superstar no longer with us is Diana Dors. She came to Newport to open the new premises of Solent Windows. There was hope that Diana could spare a few minutes for a quick chat. Three different times were set and each subsequently cancelled. In the end her assistant rang to say Diana was just too tired for an interview and was resting.

I had wasted at least four hours chasing an interview and was not too amused. For the rest of that busy Saturday I was determined to write a piece in the *Post*, complaining how much I'd been messed around. A straight 'no' is always much more acceptable than being left in limbo. By the end of the following day I'd decided to write nothing. I'd always had great admiration for Diana Dors.

Just a week or two later the news of Diana's cancer was splashed over all the papers. She had obviously, bravely, been honouring engagements, despite not feeling well. The last thing she would have wanted was an interview. I was so saddened by the news of her subsequent death and relieved I had not written that piece.

How must that Sunday newspaper journalist have felt the day Princess Diana died? She had written a scathing piece on Diana and, obviously, it had gone to print just before her tragic accident. Why did she write it anyway? I've interviewed a few people who were lucky enough to have met Diana. They will never forget that experience and were so thrilled to have had the opportunity.

My strike rate for interviews has always been around 80 per cent. Naturally, there are occasions when famous people just don't wish to be interviewed. Some are not interested, others try and tie it in with a new record, book or television show, other stars are just too busy or, in reality, I might not be high-profile enough for them. I always turn down the chance of 'phone or down-the-line interviews, whoever they are. That's meant I've missed some real top stars but I have no regrets at all. I've met so many more than your average local hack or radio presenter has.

Back in the '70s Larry Adler was in concert at the Sandown Pavilion. On numerous occasions I've ended up being a makeshift roadie or personal assistant. That's all a part of the service as far as I'm concerned. Names that spring to mind include the Beverley Sisters, Vince Hill, Bob Monkhouse, Errol Brown and Jimmy Tarbuck. On one memorable Sunday afternoon Caroline, Sean and myself carried in all Rolf Harris's gear. That was fine and so was he. Rolf even gave me some of his on-stage quick sketches to raise money for a local charity.

Back to the most famous harmonica player in the world. I helped carry in all his equipment but he wouldn't do an interview.

CHAPTER TEN

YOU CAN'T WIN THEM ALL

W HEN ANITA DOBSON came for a Southern Vectis promotion, at the peak of her *EastEnders* fame, her personal assistant refused all interview requests. It seemed that, in her estimation, Anita may have been a little too famous to be interviewed by mere local Isle of Wight journalists.

We were allowed to travel on the private bus around Newport and I was lucky enough to sit next to her – but no interview. I could only be her tour guide. Southern Vectis officials did try very hard on our behalf. Times have changed for Anita, since then.

I'm generally optimistic when writing to managements, agents, PR companies and individual stars for interview opportunities. A refusal never offends. If you sit and wait to be asked, it just won't happen. You need to be brave and hope for the best.

Sometimes I've found actors the most difficult to win over. Others, like my good friend Michael Sheard, will talk for ever. Meeting some of my own personal favourites, like Stratford Johns, William Lucas, Geraldine McEwan, Sir Bernard Miles, Celia Imrie, Letitia Dean, Anthony Bate, Glenda Jackson, Patrick Mower and Julian Wadham, has been very satisfying.

In more recent years I've had refusals from Joanna Lumley, Samantha Janus, Honor Blackman, Julie Christie and Penelope Keith. You can't win them all.

Sometimes it's their agents, managers, press officers or PR companies who decline the requests. In most cases, though, I've had nothing but superb co-operation from these people. Many have gone out of their way to be helpful and it's been much appreciated.

It's always such a bonus when artists have a change of heart. It happened with Val Doonican, Danny La Rue, and Cannon and Ball. They all had second thoughts and have become good friends. Stars definitely suss you out and, often, seek a second opinion from a showbiz pal or agent. I can understand their initial concern. There are some real prats who spoil it for everyone else. You need a genuine love of the business to get the best out of showbiz people.

The *Weekly Post* reflections have triggered off so many more. My fifteen years with the *Post* were rewarding in many ways. Not financially. The money received for the hours put in just didn't make it viable. I've never been driven by a greed for money. If I went to the mainland to do an interview, I lost money. Local journalism and radio isn't about money – more about enthusiasm and commitment. Money couldn't have bought my fifteen years of *Post* pleasure. It was a team effort.

Who could forget nights like those when I interviewed Jackie Pallo at Ryde Town Hall, or when I discovered that a top pop songwriter, Peter Dibbens, lived in Northwood, and a member of '70s teenie band Stevenson's Rocket, was the son of St Helens' shopkeepers.

Dickie Valentine was a great British crooner who was tragically killed in a car crash in Wales. I was thrilled to discover his former pianist, Hal Chambers, had bought a stationery shop in Seaview. Hal's daughter was also in show business, like both her mum and dad, and was married to Dick Emery. On one Bank Holiday, Heather and I popped into the shop to see Hal and Vera and were served by a guy whose face looked rather familiar – it was Dick Emery.

On June 26, 1977, there was a Gala Jubilee Show at the Sandown Pavilion, attended by the late Lord Louis Mountbatten. That was a most memorable occasion. There were hundreds waiting outside, just to see our Island Governor arrive. It set the seal on a marvellous spectacle and on the bill were Ray Alan and Lord Charles – that brought a laugh or two from Lord Louis – Hope and Keen, Freddie 'Parrot Face' Davies and John Boulter. A few years earlier I'd briefly met Lord Louis with Uffa Fox (what a double act) at a Cowes Time-Limit Cricket League presentation evening.

Alvin Stardust came to the Island and was a perfect host at Yelf's Hotel, seventy-year-old Sir Bernard Miles breezed into the Sandown Pavilion and told me he dreamed of becoming a good actor, and two *Dad's Army* stars, Ian Lavender and Bill Pertwee, were at the Sandown Rivoli cinema's Christmas party.

There were some super nights at the prison clubs and once, at Albany, Joe Brown brought his wife Vicki, once of the Vernon Girls and Breakaways, as his backing singer. What a talent! She made records in her own right and, as a session singer, helped others to fame. Once again, Vicki was a singer whose life was drastically cut short. Many years later, at Sandown, the likeable Cockney sang a new song, *Come On Joe*, that everyone thought Joe had written about his late wife. It was so poignant and he performed it with such feeling. It was not his song but the lyric summed up everyone's thoughts.

Frank Bough enjoyed a one-nighter at the Pavilion and introduced a questions and answer segment. He was the *Grandstand* TV host and a punter asked him about *World Of Sport*, the rival ITV show. He answered: "I really don't know much about that show. I'm usually a little busy at that time."

I was tipped off that Antonia Ellis, from Newport, was back home from America for a short visit. Her mother sent me a kind invitation to join them at home. Toni, the daughter of the late Martin Ellis, the former Island bandleader, had appeared in Ken Russell's movie *The Boyfriend* and starred on Broadway and in the West End. She appeared in seventeen episodes of *UFO* and was even seen as a stripper in that hilarious movie, *Percy*. In 1979 she was nominated for the West End's Top Musical Actress award.

Two local boys came back to the Island for short visits. Les Payne, who had tried to become a pop star for over thirty years, and one who had succeeded, Snowy White. You could form a real supergroup of Island-born musicians. These two would make an impact – Les a great singer and songwriter and

Snowy such a celebrated guitarist. Another welcome homecoming was for Roy Colegate, once of local band Five Alive. He'd gone off to Scandinavia, like Snowy White. Roy stayed and joined a famous folk-rock Swedish band called Scafell Pike. It was a different world to La Babalu, the old Ryde nightclub, and zany DJ Malc Lawrence.

Brad Newman had become something of a cult figure during the late '60s at Sandown's Vancouver Bar. The place was packed out every night for Brad's unique style of vocal and keyboard rock 'n' roll. He came back in the '70s to other local venues. He'd always had a great local following. Brad, who had toured with Cliff Richard and included some of the Beatles among his fans, did make several pop singles, one of which, *Somebody To Love*, made the Top 50.

He returned to the Island in '78 to play a season at The Holliers, Shanklin. That summer he was a hit with the nearby Shanklin Theatre company and Bob Grant, Jack from TV's *On The Buses*, was so impressed he teamed up with Brad to write a musical, *A Legend For The Future*. The futuristic idea was excellent and Brad's music brought it all to life. Sadly, it never saw the light of day.

Bob Grant and Brad Newman wrote a musical on the Island. Now, here's the plot, John ...

Brad died in Spain during late 1998. Such a talent, who never really fulfilled his true potential – but was happy enough entertaining in pubs and clubs. We gave him a good send-off with an Isle of Wight Radio tribute show that proved very popular. Brad would have loved it. Dave Bambrough, from Lake, also found some rare local recordings for the show.

Being invited to the Cliff Tops to meet Cecil Landeau was indeed an honour. I did enjoy chatting to such a world-famous impresario. Stars like Audrey Hepburn, Max Bygraves, Norman Wisdom, Eartha Kitt and Danny La Rue owed a great deal to his vision.

When Jimmy Cricket invited me down to Sandown to chat to his agent, it was another chance to meet a person who had discovered a world-famous talent. Phyllis Rounce had first seen the potential in Tony Hancock and had guided him to fame. In succeeding years, Tony was known for pushing aside those who'd done most for him, like Phyllis, Simpson and Galton, and Sid James.

Don Duval was always a useful contact for me. During the early '70s, when I was writing for the *Wightman*, he was presenting shows on Shanklin Pier. Among those he booked were Ronnie Carroll and Ruby Murray. Later, when he'd moved to St Lawrence, Don 'phoned to invite me to meet an old pal of his, Malcolm Roberts, that big-voice pop star with hits like *Love Is All*. Don Duval, a performer himself, did a great version of Elvis's *Wooden Heart*.

In 1979 Frank Ifield was one of the stars booked for the Memorial Hall, Freshwater. Those West Wight nights were nothing short of magical. So many stars appeared, including Roy Castle, The Bevs, The Searchers, Wout Steenhuis, Marty Wilde, Joe Brown, Helen Shapiro, Kenny Ball, Acker Bilk and the Tremeloes, with an all original line-up. The hospitality was fantastic and John and Pat Howe were extremely obliging. Sean and I had a great hour with Joe Brown in the nearby Prince of Wales pub. Frank Ifield, which is where I came in, brought out the house-full boards and saved the show. There was a power failure for close on an hour and he sat with his guitar and a torch to entertain during the blackout. I'll remember you, Frank.

Some of the Ponda Rosa's most successful nights were the rock 'n' roll specials. Matchbox were always popular, with their excellent singer Graham Fenton. Within a couple of months of their Ashey gig, the band were in the pop charts with *Rockabilly Rebel*, the first of their eight hits. I've often kept in touch with Graham since that first interview.

Chas 'n' Dave also came just before their big chart breakthrough. This was for a private gig at the Savoy Country Club, for the guests of Courage's. It was just for a few customers and was a rather special night. They had three huge Top 10 hits a year or two later.

On another occasion at the Savoy I met author Leslie Thomas of *Virgin Soldiers* fame who'd come over for a public appearance. He was relieved to sneak away from the action to record an interview with me.

Over Easter of 1979 my long-time friend Mick Bull, who had a superb book called *Keep It On The Island*, tracing the history of local football, published in 1998, rang up to say Don Lang, once of *Six-Five Special* fame, was staying at a private house in Shanklin and I could go and have a chat. That was a great experience. He actually recorded the theme of the innovative television series.

Earlier we talked of warm-up acts who go on before the big stars to help build up the atmosphere. Sometimes they can be accomplished performers in their own right. Many have lost jobs simply because they are too strong for the top-of-the-bill acts. Other than the early days of Brian Conley and Wayne Dobson, the greatest support I ever saw at Sandown was Peter Goodwright.

He came in the summer of 1980 and virtually stole the show every night, whoever the star he was supporting. Afterwards he would slip away from Sandown Pier in his old mac. That man was just brilliant. Peter made his name on the radio, when they had really funny comedy shows. That was some time ago, with the exception of the *News Huddlines*.

One night after the show, in Peter's dressing room, we were drinking lime juice and chatting away when a knock came at the door. It was a lady patiently waiting for an autograph. She gleefully accepted a signed picture from Peter and said: "I thought you were brilliant." I seconded that but she suddenly turned to me and remarked: "And you were very good too." There was a deadly hush until she left and then we fell about laughing. We were both intrigued to know who she actually thought I was in the show but we never found out. I don't think it was Frankie Howerd. "Get your titters out madam," is hardly me.

Talking to Lennie Bennett, whilst he was under the shower, and a marvellous night with Arthur Mullard, when he came for a personal appearance at the Newport Bingo and Social Club, are other memorable moments that come to mind. Arthur took me over to Calvert's for a quiet drink. Then a well-oiled customer spotted him. "Watch this, I'll get a drink out of that drunk," promised Arthur. The guy made a nuisance of himself and Arthur waited his time, before saying: "I'll have a double whisky." It worked a treat.

In the '70s and early '80s there were often top names at the Medina Theatre. It was quite novel to turn the tables on *Desert Island Discs* host Roy Plombley and ask him to choose his eight favourite records, and to come face to face with a real comedy genius, Eric Sykes. Knowing he was deaf, I tried to make it easy and asked him which side I should sit to interview him. "Don't worry, I've got my glasses on," replied Eric. This augured well for our interview. Then I twigged. Eric had a minute hearing aid set in his spectacle frames and could hear from any angle. Whoops!

Current pop stars rarely appear on the Island. During the chart success of Bronski Beat, their founder, Steve Bronski, came to Newport to visit pop photographer Michael Morton. His mother, Elizabeth, is a super lady and I was invited to visit their house to meet Steve.

Where are your glasses, Eric?
Can you hear me?

CHAPTER ELEVEN

YANKS, SOAPS & SEAN WHO?

MIKE STICKLAND, at Warner's Puckpool, was the first holiday centre manager in Britain to pioneer cabaret and special pop week-ends. His experiments with acts like the Stylistics, Ben E. King, who even did an impromptu gig at the nearby Battery, Jimmy Ruffin, the Drifters and the Crickets, was the signal for other British leisure centres to follow suit. Another surprise act at the centre were the Ink Spots, who included Jim Nabbie, who had joined the American group back in '45. What a columnist's dream they were, too, all those American acts.

There were a number of notable British stars who performed at Puckpool, including that fantastic singer Tony Christie, who made a come-back to the pop charts in the late '90s. This was his first appearance at a holiday centre and Puckpool was not as modern as today's Harcourt Sands complex, which is an amalgamation of the old Puckpool and St Clare camps. Tony dubbed the entertainment's room the 'Commandant's office' as it looked out over the chalets. It reminded him of a PoW camp and was a world away from all those glittering '70s nightclubs he'd worked, like the Batley Variety Club and Cæsar's Palace, Luton. Tony parked his Rolls Royce, TON10, outside the hamburger stall.

Others who came to Puckpool included Guys and Dolls. In their line-up was Julie Forsyth, Bruce's daughter. I can remember telling her that one of my dreams was to interview her father. Twenty years on that dream was to become reality.

When Marty Wilde came he reflected on the first visit he'd made to Puckpool, over thirty years earlier. He'd travelled there on a bus with his parents and didn't even win the weekly talent contest. He came second. Mind you, he was just plain Reg Smith, schoolboy, at the time. On his next visit he was driving a Mercedes 5000. This time he rang his mother from the car 'phone. That's rock 'n' roll for you.

There was an unforgettable night for me at the Wishing Well in November 1982. Without any pre-publicity the Cherokees, one of the best-loved of the Island's home-grown bands, decided to re-form for just the one night. Pondwell had never seen anything like it. There were cars everywhere and police directing traffic and trying to sort out the parking. Residents on the nearby estate weren't too happy. Inside the pub everyone was more than happy. The boys, a term I use loosely, were in fine form and had been rehearsing for the gig. There were so many in the Wishing Well, with a queue that stretched down the hill. As people left others were allowed in. That was another scoop. There was no pre-publicity, so who told the punters?

Just up the hill, in Seaview, I went to rediscover an old shopkeeper friend, Oliver Smallman. Many years previous, during my days as a salesman, I'd called on Wroxall Stores, then owned by Ollie. We became great mates. When he sold the shop in 1973, because of the introduction of VAT, the grocer's nightmare, and left the Island, we lost contact. Ten years later he was Britain's top record plugger.

One of his greatest successes was working on Wings' *Mull of Kintyre*, which sold nearly three millions copies and earnt Ollie his reputation. Pluggers make hits. He excelled with Clout's *Substitute* and then went to work on Dollar, with amazing success. Latterly he has moved into the management business and looked after the British interests of Imagination, Stevie Wonder, Kim Carnes and Lionel Richie. His Yardrose Promotions company also made records, including *I'm Alright*, with Steve Wright.

The last I heard of him he was doing even better – managing Eternal and Louise. Now someone works his VAT out for him.

Keith Newbery once tipped me off about a story from a dancing school. I'm almost certain his daughter was a pupil there. The lady's name was Ann Stephanie from the Footlights School, Leed Street, Sandown.

When I went to see Ann she revealed she was in the new jumbo dancing troupe, the Roly-Polys, formed for the Les Dawson television series. In a similar vein to the Spice Girls, many years later, Ann answered an advert in *The Stage*, to audition for a new dance group. Joining the Roly-Polys was to change her life for ever. I used to get cards and letters sent by her from all over the world.

Billie Jo Spears came for a Sandown one-nighter and 1,500 saw her two shows. The original recorder of hits like *Blanket on the Ground* and *'57 Chevrolet* really pulled in the crowds. There was a backstage crisis because she had unexpected throat problems and the second show was almost pulled. Somehow she got through that second house and no-one knew of her plight – until the next *Weekly Post*.

Her English-born husband Doug was very protective and would not allow an interview. With her throat problems, it was not surprising. Three hours later, surprisingly, he changed his mind and Billie Jo came in for a chat. Billie also went into the audience and asked questions. That was another historic night at the Pavilion.

Scottish tenor Kenneth McKellar came for a summer at the Shanklin Theatre. This was a prestigious booking for the theatre as Kenneth was very popular. What a gentlemen, too. On the very last night he invited me to his dressing room to present me with a book on Scotland, personally signed by him. That gesture really took me by surprise.

Whilst Kenneth was here for the whole summer, he walked into a Ventnor bank and was instantly recognised. As he left, the cashier remarked: "Have a nice holiday on the Isle of Wight, Mr McKellar." Well, I suppose that Shanklin is all of four miles from Ventnor. News doesn't always travel fast. I'm not sure if that bank had even heard about decimalisation.

Brian McDermott, a very strange man but a fine actor, came to the Island and converted the Prince Consort, Ryde, into a theatre. I admired his determination and confidence but not always his projects, ideas and choices of productions. Brian, always a caring host, invited me to the Consort to meet a virtually unknown young actor called Ian Reddington, who was about to join a pop group, Heaven 17. Then he was starring in *The Collector* at Ryde. Years later he emerged as Tricky Dicky on *EastEnders*.

In 1984 I met Ruby Murray for the first time. She had been my mother's favourite singer and had set a record that no-one else has ever equalled – five singles in the same Top Twenty chart. If she could have done that in more recent years, Ruby would never have needed to work again. How different it was in the '50s. She earnt fabulous money but was seen off by crooked businessmen and forced to sell her lovely home just to pay her tax bill. Unfortunately Ruby was rather naïve and didn't even sense she was being ripped off.

'50s superstar Ruby Murray and singing son Tim.

It was sad to think she was now doing the *Sun* bingo to try and win some money. A lady of her international status, even known by Frank Sinatra, should never have drifted into this way of life. I really felt very sorry for her. Ruby, a gem of a lady, was not looking for sympathy. She was enjoying life and still singing well. Years later she came to the Isle of Wight just to appear on my radio show, with her singing son, Tim. Still as nervous as ever, she held on to me for the whole show. Ruby died a year or two back.

It was in 1985 that I went to Havenstreet Station to meet one of TV's most suave and popular presenters, David Icke. At that time he was looking for a house on the Island. A lot has happened since those days. I've always enjoyed David's company and that of his wonderful wife, Linda.

When David was going through his high-profile religious campaign, I stood next to him at a Jethro concert – and was not sure when to laugh or what to laugh at. He certainly found it very funny. David Icke has always treated me fairly. As a television sports presenter he was quite brilliant.

You meet all sorts in show business. I've always enjoyed comedians. Some are full of surprises, none more than Charlie Smithers. I caught up with him during his Island season for Warners and discovered he had an unusual hobby, visiting local graveyards. His aim was to find the oldest gravestones. He discovered one in Arreton that was 750 years old. His jokes were never that vintage, though, honestly.

The Brat, who made that 1982 *Chalkdust* hit record, suggesting that John McEnroe didn't always play fair, turned up for a one-nighter at the Ventnor Winter Gardens and confessed to being Roger Kitter – comedian, impressionist and actor. We have stayed good friends ever since.

I never knew Nick Dingley, known to millions of world-wide rock fans as Razzle. Nick, a former pupil of Mayfield Middle and Ryde High schools, had made it big-time in Hanoi Rocks, a Finnish rock band with a great reputation and several exciting albums. It was a sad day on December 8, 1984, when this young Islander was killed in a Los Angeles car crash. His parents, Henry and Irene, from Binstead, received over 200 sympathy cards from all over the world. At his local funeral there were a hundred mainland mourners and sixty floral tributes, including wreaths from Cyndi Lauper, Girlschool and Twisted Sister. Closer to home, there was one from Binstead Scouts, where he had learnt to play drums. Before heading for London to seek pop fame, Nick had worked at Ryde's Belle Vue Garage.

His heartbroken parents were keen to contribute to a *Stage Talk* tribute, which also celebrated the life of the twenty-four-year-old Islander.

Ironically, in a Finnish pop music paper a few months before his accident, there was a feature on Hanoi Rocks. The only English content in the feature arose from a piece about Razzle. It simply said: "Too fast to live, too young to die."

Another father so proud of his rock star son was David Kossoff. Paul was the inspirational guitarist with Free, who actually played at the 1970 Isle of Wight Pop Festival. Paul had also died long before his time. When I went to meet David Kossoff at the Medina Theatre, Newport, he proved to be such a delightful man but did not wish to talk about his late son, who'd been a guitar icon to many youngsters.

In order to acknowledge his wishes I kept well away from the subject. David, himself, had such a fascinating story. I'd first listened to him on *Journey Into Space* on the Light Programme. During our conversation, David suddenly decided he wanted to talk about Paul and he paid him such a touching tribute. Ever the caring father, he also went on to praise the talents of other members of his family.

Over the years there have been several show business football matches on the Island. One Sunday back in the '50s, when the famous Showbiz XI came to Church Litten, Newport, Tommy Steele and Sean Connery were in their line-up. The ultimate James Bond was then quite unknown but still got the ladies excited – particularly in shorts.

When the Showbiz XI returned, this time to Westwood Park, Cowes, in 1984, I walked into their dressing room and saw this huge figure with 'Rick Wakeman World Tour' on his T-shirt. When he turned around, it was the rock superstar himself. We've had a few meetings since then and he's appeared live on my radio show on numerous occasions. Once he even brought in his ex-model wife, Nina Carter. That was some Sunday lunchtime. Rick's an amazing guy, having fought off several heart attacks.

Returning to celebrity football, I was asked to pick a John Hannam XI to take on the TV Entertainers at Westridge, in April of 1985. We hammered them out of sight in a most enjoyable afternoon. I was able to choose a team of local footballers I'd really admired over the years. It included the likes of Barry Allen, Tony Grimwade, Chris Cheverton and John Carragher.

There were several *Coronation Street* stars in their side, including Nigel Pivaro, who plays Terry Duckworth, and Michael Le Vell, who is loved by *'Street* fans as Kevin Webster. They and all their team mates were excellent opponents.

There was a great Michael Le Vell story. The TV Entertainers' coach broke down going out of Portsmouth and someone suggested Michael, alias Kevin the motor mechanic in the soap, should have a look a it. Apparently, he didn't have a clue, much to the delight of his team mates. They had to send for a real mechanic.

The other major match was when the *EastEnders* cast came down, under the guise of the Walford Boy's Club XI, to play the Island's Glen Moreton XI. Glen was a very talented Island swimmer who met with a serious diving accident, in June 1987. He became paralysed and restricted to a wheelchair. A young man of great courage – as he's gone on to prove. Over 3,000 turned up to watch at St George's Park. At the pre-match reception, the TV stars admitted they'd been celebrating Nick Berry's birthday, the night before.

The Island team had many good local players in it and I was just there as a sub. It was a nice way to say 'thanks' for a large publicity campaign. Before the game, superbly organised by Barry Groves, we were told not to tackle hard or rough-up the opposition. They were working actors who had to be back in the studios the following morning. Imagine our surprise when they tore into the Glen Moreton team as if their lives depended on it. Adam Woodyatt (Ian Beale) was a right dirty little so and so, and one of the home team suddenly seemed to slow him down a little. Local player Oscar Stretch was taken off because he was getting too excited. It was more like an old Brading v Seaview game.

In the end the *EastEnders'* stars, who also included Tom Watt (Lofty), Nick Berry (Wicksy), Mick Gardner (Tel), Gary Webster (Graham) and Gary Macdonald (Darren), just about took a rare defeat. It was great fun and a lot of money was raised for local charities. I was delighted to interview Tom Watt – before the game. That was a shrewd move. It was quite a day. That night I also interviewed football manager Tommy Docherty, and Colin Milburn, the ex-England cricketer, at Newport's Medina Theatre.

What are you doing here? That could apply to many stars and personalities who have turned up on the Isle of Wight over the past thirty years or so. Perhaps you can remember some of these.

The famous movie actor Simon Ward, the star of hit films like *Young Winston*, *Aces High*, *Four Feathers* and *All Creatures Great and Small*, arrived at the Sandown Pavilion in the midst of winter. He was here to star in the Ivor Novello musical *Perchance To Dream*. It was a rare opportunity to see a top professional company on your own doorstep, without going to Chichester or Southsea. What a fantastic stage show, and Simon Ward was magnificent. Not too many realised that, though. On opening night there were just sixty-eight in the theatre. On some other nights there were more on stage than in the auditorium. It was an insult to such a fantastic company. They were the smallest audiences of their eighteen-week national tour.

It was hard for the company to hide their obvious disappointment – although it was Sandown in deepest winter. Simon, still as youthful as ever, tried to soften the embarrassment: "Why should those who have taken the trouble to come, suffer? It's not their fault others stayed away." The company played as if it was to a full house. The next two weeks, at Wimbledon and Darlington, were sell-outs. They'd earnt that.

Letitia Dean, who played Sharon in *EastEnders*, turned up at Puckpool, to open the Island Motor Show. Then, one autumn week-end in Cowes, along came Barbara Windsor and Gareth Hunt for the finals of the J24 class sailing championships. What a bonus to pick up three unexpected interviews. I was just a little more excited talking to Barbara and Letitia than to Mr Hunt. Sorry Gareth.

World famous musical and pop writer Tim Rice was tempted by Ryde High School to come and watch their production of *Blondel*. That must have taken some persuasion. He was most impressed and happy to talk and mingle.

Another person always prepared to talk was Brian Johnston, better known as 'Johners', the mercurial broadcaster. I've been lucky enough to interview

both him and John Arlott. What legends to share a mike with. Brian was reported to be in Yarmouth recording a *Down Your Way*. At the end of the day he was happy to sit and chat over a nice cup of flavoured tea. In the end we did our interview

The master and apprentice at Yarmouth. Earl Grey came next.

70

overlooking the harbour and were even photographed by a few visitors. When John Arlott came to Newport's Medina Theatre he seemed very tired. Now we only have memories of them both.

Bobby Moore was a world soccer hero, liked everywhere he went, and one of those few players who performed even better for England than he did for his own club, West Ham. Bobby was such a gentle man and it was nothing short of an honour and a privilege to go and meet him at Buywise, Newport, where he was making a personal appearance. He was so nice to my young daughter. What would he be worth in today's over-inflated football market? There will never be another like him.

A real football icon – Bobby Moore at Buywise, Newport.

In the '80s stunt ace Eddie Kidd actually came to undertake a one-nighter at Bogey's. At that time he fancied himself as a pop star, a career which never materialised. Hale and Pace also came to the Sandown Pavilion when they were just emerging as new comedy stars. They were soon one of the hottest pairings in the business. The boys were so inventive in those days, even on a small portable tape recorder.

I also caught up with Shane Richie during his visit for the end-of-season night at Whitecliff Bay Holiday Park. He had to work hard that night. Shane was just beginning to break into the top flight. Many years earlier he'd been a blue coat at Pontin's, Little Canada.

"Why didn't you come and see me when I was at Pontin's, Little Canada?" teased Shane. I probably had, to interview visiting star cabarets, but never noticed him. Although that's hard to imagine. Such a multi-talented entertainer. We met again in August 1999, when he was starring in *Boogie Nights*. From that same show I also interviewed Grace Kennedy. That produced another hot flush – mine, of course.

During the '80s I also finally caught up with ex-local rock 'n' roll star Johnny Vincent. In the '50s and '60s he'd been very popular on the Island. Many local fans wanted to know where he was. In the end I tracked him down to Andover. Amazingly, his son was my milkman at that time and I had no idea. The name Mowbray – Vincent was Johnny's stage name – just didn't register. Michael's mum and dad had split up.

CHAPTER TWELVE

RADIO BREAKTHROUGH

I N THE '80s I had my first taste of public radio. The local hospital radio network can only be heard by patients. This can prove disappointing for presenters, in some cases, because so much enthusiasm and effort is put into programmes.

I'd been a Radio Solent listener since day one, particularly for their unrivalled sports coverage. Some of their presenters like Jeff Link, Richard Cartridge, Bill Buckley, Dennis Skillicorn, Ian Henderson and Pam Gillard had been particular favourites of mine. When invited to join their Saturday morning panel to judge new record releases, I jumped at the chance. I was asked to provide two more local panellists to link up with their mainland studio, from their small Newport Quay Street studio. I co-opted local mobile DJ Dave Cass and hospital radio broadcaster Carol Fry. I think we followed *Albert's Gang*. I'm not sure if that was good or bad.

On one occasion I invited in Denise Nolan from Jimmy Tarbuck's Sandown Pavilion show, to be a guest reviewer. We had a coffee in God's Providence and suddenly realised we should be on air. I think we got away with being late. It was a self-service studio. You had to set it all up yourself. That welcome experience whetted my appetite for radio. One or two other local radio presenters owe a lot to Solent.

A few years later, Jean-Paul Hansford and Steve Oates saw the fruition of their dream. In March 1990 came the opening of Isle of Wight Radio, a commercial station on medium wave. There had been a fight for the franchise and one or two other interested parties suffered a little wounded pride. There were excellent people in the other groups, too. Some were to eventually join forces with the franchise winners. I'd also been alerted that the other bidders were keen for me to work for them. Much of the real spade work for an Island community station had been undertaken by Pat Norris. He was the real instigator and worked very hard with the Radio Authority and other important people.

Several months earlier there had been ideas for a sort of *Stage Talk* on Isle of Wight Radio. Both founders were keen to follow up the prospect. Since my hospital radio days and subsequent *Weekly Post* years, I'd always interviewed all the stars on tape, for several reasons. Many were played on Isle of Wight Hospital Radio and they also formed a library for future *Post* interviews. Once on tape, you could take the notes when required. On occasions I had as much as three months *Stage Talks* on tape.

Some of these interviews were listened to by Jean-Paul and Steve, despite a few being hastily recorded as pure newspaper stories. They were always conducted as proper start and end interviews. This led directly to the initial offer of *John Hannam Meets*.

In the end I wondered if the offer would ever come to fruition. The station opened on Easter Sunday of 1990 and it was not until the following Thursday that Steve Oates' offer was confirmed for an hour-long interview slot, within his Saturday night show. I had all of two days notice.

Bernie Cullen, the lead singer of Five Alive and a notable Island sportsman, plus local show promoter Peter Brennen, were hastily recruited as the first night live guests. My initial spot was 9 to 10 p.m. on a Saturday night. Within a couple of weeks it was taken out of Steve's show, which was shortened by an hour. It was given the same slot, as *John Hannam Meets*.

Some of the early guests included a few stars from the Sandown Pavilion. Martin Daniels and Les Dennis came in live. I was also their taxi service, to and from the theatre where they were rehearsing. Hundreds of guests have followed and some I still can't believe were actually on my show. It just shouldn't have happened on one of Britain's tiniest radio stations.

I owe a lot to Jean-Paul, who often wrote congratulatory letters after shows, which was very satisfying, and to Steve Oates. It was their brainchild. Over the years I've had notable production support from Bill Padley, Stuart McGinley, Charlie Brook, Richard Pocock, Ian Mac, Tom Stroud, Dominic Green and Duncan Smith. Most of the other presenters have consistently given me their encouragement, help and time. That's been much appreciated. The station's Island directors have always been very supportive to me.

The show was moved to Sunday lunch-times in January 1991. This was to prove a very popular time. I'm extremely grateful to the thousands who listened every week. We built up a very loyal following and the feedback was quite amazing.

These days Mike Osman is one of the South's most popular broadcasters. In many respects his listening figures are higher than those of rival national broadcasters, within the same area. He came over from Southampton to do a live Sunday show. That was long before his own radio aspirations. For much of that show Mike was impersonating Lawrie McMenemy, then the Southampton Director of Football, and it was so realistic many thought it was actually Lawrie who was on the show with me. Unbeknown to Mike, I'd arranged for the real Lawrie McMenemy to 'phone in during the programme. That turned out to be a riot of fun and Mike Osman was almost lost for words.

Jim Smith is a football figure I have a lot of time for. The so-called glamour managers who are often more interested in medallions, trendy clothes and the latest dolly bird on their arm, than in running football teams, leave me absolutely cold. Men like Ron Atkinson and Malcolm Allison have always been more interested in fuelling their own egos. Give me honest down-to-earth workers like Jim Smith, Alan Ball, Martin O'Neill and Dave Jones any day of the week.

Jim Smith was due at Ryde for a guest appearance at the Royal York dinner of the Island Portsmouth Supporters' Club. I popped in late on the Saturday night to confirm that Jim was okay for the following morning. The Pompey boss was in high spirits, in more ways than one. I was suddenly worried that Jim might just not be up to an hour's live radio the very next morning. What an old pro! He was on time, having the perfect chauffeur in Henry Adams, and in superb form. I was so grateful that Jim delayed his return to his Oxford home to appear live on the show.

A few years later, when he'd moved to Derby County, he allowed me into the club's Friday night hotel, in Fareham, to talk to Island boy Gary Rowett, on the eve of their Premiership match at the Dell.

On December 20, 1992, we made a little national radio history. Footballer James Lawrence, who was then in Camphill Prison, was released for an hour to appear live on my show. It was all a part of his

Would Jim Smith be fit for a Sunday lunchtime live interview after a night out on the Isle of Wight?

rehabilitation programme, arranged by Eddie Walder. His appearance did upset a few listeners but we picked up more praise than criticism. James made a pledge on air to go straight and to try and make big-time football. At that time, also, he was playing for Cowes Sports.

There was a happy ending and several on the Island deserve praise for that. He's now an established professional footballer, having played for Sunderland, Leicester City, Doncaster and Bradford. Good luck to you, Jamie.

I'll never forget the day Bobby Stokes came in live on the show. It was May 8, 1994, and he was playing in an afternoon charity match at St George's Park. Bob still seemed mesmerised by all the world fame he created by scoring the winning goal in the 1976 FA Cup Final, when Southampton beat Manchester United 1-0. Such a lovely, unspoilt man. Sadly, he died a year or two later.

English sport enthusiasts have long been impressed by the cricketing antics of Ian Botham, one of the greatest ever sporting heroes of the masses. When he came to Ventnor Winter Gardens for a one-nighter he wasn't at all interested in an interview.

In August, 1993, his son, Liam, certainly was up for an interview. At that time he was making a few appearances for Ventnor and came into the studio the day after they had won the Island's Knock-Out Cup. What a delight he turned out to be. Young Mark Garaway, who's done me several real favours, set it all up. Liam also made a promise that the next time he appeared on my show he wouldn't wear the previous night's T-shirt, with all the curry stains very much in evidence.

Another embarrassing moment happened in the manager's office of Southampton Football Club. Ian Branfoot had willingly agreed to an interview but my tape recorder would have none of it. Ian rang the genial John Hughes from Radio Solent, a marvellous broadcaster, who willingly brought up his machine. There was an unexpected ending. Ian decided that he and his wife would enjoy a quiet week-end on the Island.

So the plan was for me to set it all up and he would then appear live on a Sunday lunch-time. The honeymoon suite was duly booked at the Swainston Manor Hotel, Calbourne. That was the least I could do. Ian invited me to the Saints' Saturday match against Aston Villa, with a seat in the director's box. At the pre-match reception in the board room I met two ardent Villa fans, ace violinist Nigel Kennedy and their former winger Peter McPartland. Saints won 2-0, against all the odds, and poor old Nigel was completely shell-shocked.

After the game, Ian Branfoot ran me down to the ferry and brought his car over. He was almost mobbed by happy Saints fans on the ferry. That was an unexpected bonus for him, particularly at that time. That memorable week-end was all due to a broken Uher tape machine.

On the day of the original meeting with Ian at the Dell, I had an afternoon appointment with David Essex at the Mayflower Theatre. This had to be postponed. David was most understanding and invited me back two days later. On

that occasion I borrowed Pat Norris' tape machine. That was the signal to invest in a DAT tape recorder and you can get up to three hours on the same side of the tape. On the Uher it was around fourteen minutes, if you were lucky.

I was to meet up with David a year or two later here on the Island – this time in the offices of Robin Hill, where the hospitality was first class. David Essex is such a great guy. He still has great memories of filming *That'll Be The Day* here on the Island.

David, can I come back in two days time?

76

CHAPTER THIRTEEN

NORMAN CONQUERS &
SIR CLIFF PLAYS HOST

L IVE, IN-PERSON chat shows can be stressful but there are many magical
moments that can only occur with this kind of show. When Bernie
Clifton came in live, it was a Sunday lunch-time when they were
resurfacing the St Mary's roundabout. It was nothing short of chaotic – inside
and outside the studio. He'd taken longer to get from Parkhurst to Dodnor
than he had to get across he Solent. That incident led to an hour's utter
mayhem.

Through a few mutual friends I tempted Norman Wisdom to come in on
September 27, 1992. Could I cope? Just about, was the eventual summary.
Norman began by reading the weather, a quiet enough start – or was it? It was
all invented. He took so long the music bed had long run out. Then it was
another hour of wonderful madness. In contrast, there were also some really
serious moments when Norman revealed how he was beaten as a child.

After the radio show, Norman was due to perform the re-opening cere-
mony for the Frank James Hospital at East Cowes. The town had not seen
crowds like it since the previous Cowes Fireworks night. The hospital grounds
were teeming with people and even Norman became a little frightened – and
he'd been mobbed all over the world! Everyone wanted to get near him. In the
end, for his safety, he asked me to take him inside. That doesn't happen too
much on the Island.

Norman Wisdom – jester supreme – at Frank James' Hospital.
(Picture by kind permission of the Isle of Wight County Press)

During that autumn period, the Earl Mountbatten Hospice was also in temporary residence at Frank James. What happened after we were inside I will never forget. Norman wanted to go in and chat to the Hospice patients. He burst in and visually seemed to be inspired by some inner strength. He made a fuss of all the patients and kissed the ladies, joked with the men and virtually did a stage show in front of them. Their reactions brought tears to everyone's eyes, except Norman. He was clearly affected by it but no-one would have guessed. He just couldn't have broken down. To see those unfortunate people so happy in Norman Wisdom's company was one of the most touching moments I have ever witnessed. There could never have been a Norman Wisdom over-hype. He is a genius, a legend, a supreme professional – and one of the most charismatic stars Britain has ever had.

On the way back to the hotel, before his evening show at Sandown, I drove Norman to see old friends of his at Ryde, Billy Whittaker and Mimi Law. To get there he insisted I took a route along country lanes rather than on the main roads. That tea-time session was yet another side of Norman Wisdom – jester to his own colleagues.

Billy Whittaker, sadly now no longer with us, was a real treasure. My two young people loved him like a grandfather. As a pantomime dame he was in the country's top three. With Mimi, they were the perfect partnership – on and off stage. Stars like Norman and Ken Dodd queued up for Billy's services supporting them in top Christmas seasons.

During the latter end of 1993 I noticed a person waiting in reception at the end of my lunch-time show. He introduced himself as Vic Farrow, the owner of Lake's Screen De Luxe cinema, and readily admitted he was a great fan of the show. Then came one of the greatest questions I have ever been asked. "Would you like to interview Cliff Richard?" This was too good to be true. My initial reaction was that I'd been set up by a fellow presenter. Then Vic produced a briefcase with several pictures showing him with Cliff. He quickly explained that his company, Direct Line Insurance, was sponsor of the Cliff Richard Tennis Trail, which encourages young hopefuls. Vic added: "If you can be at home this Thursday around 1 p.m., I'll call you from Cliff's offices."

I made sure I was there and the anticipated call came in from Cliff's manager, Bill Latham. "So you want to come up and talk to Cliff?" was his opening line. A date was set there and then. This really was a dream come true.

There was a wait of around five weeks during which I tried not to get too excited. I was also intent on keeping it a secret from everyone, except my family. Even the radio station were not aware. During the last few days I did have several sleepless nights. Mostly with the recurring theme of what could go wrong – and what if it did? Say I was ill, or the tape recorder didn't work? It was agony. The day eventually came and I awoke early. I sat up in bed and remember talking aloud to myself. "John, this is a big day for you, so don't let yourself down. If you cock it up, you'll regret it for the rest of your life." That dose of self-induced confidence did the trick. I was flying.

Vic even came to Godshill to pick me up and took me personally to Cliff's Surrey offices, where there were thirty people working for him. As we climbed the stairs Cliff came running down. "You must be John," he enquired. I nearly replied, "You must be Cliff," but managed to save myself. I had bought *Move It* right back in September '58 and had been a fan ever since.

A few minutes later we were in the interview room and I was setting up. Then came the bombshell. I'll set the scene. I'd hoped for an hour of Cliff's time to turn it into a two-hour special and had planned the interview meticulously for that duration, with at least ten records to compliment the chat. So, back to that Surrey morning. Bill Latham suddenly knocked my confidence for six. "Cliff's running late and we can only spare fifteen minutes," said Bill.

I was completely drained as I prepared for our chat and Cliff must have sensed I looked a little harassed and asked if I was okay. I'd probably gone white and I could feel my mouth was completely dry. Perhaps he noticed, too, that I was shaking. I mumbled that I could do with a drink. Two minutes later Cliff returned with a tray, bottled water and glasses. Here was Cliff Richard waiting on me. My inner voice was now trying to calm my situation.

Then the interview started and we'd been left in this comfy room on our own. Within minutes my nerves had vanished, there was an instant rapport between us and I could feel the adrenaline rush. Cliff was clearly enjoying it – and so was I. There's a timer clock on my tape recorder and the minutes were ticking by. I was suddenly willing myself to keep going.

I had seen a couple of faces at the window but no intrusion. When the clock had reached 47 minutes, I decided I ought to call a halt and not blot my copybook. It was a little over those fifteen minutes.

A day or two earlier I'd worked out an idea for a trailer to advertise Cliff's appearance on my show – and typed a script for each of us. Would he do it? He'd obviously enjoyed our interview and was in the perfect mood. I asked him if he would consider doing a trailer to plug the show. He looked at the script and loved the idea. The plan was for us to sing a duet and he would tease me about my voice.

Take one worked like a dream but Cliff actually got my name wrong. I had to ask for take number two – and it was perfect.

Armed with prizes for *County Press* and Isle of Wight Radio competitions, he signed everything

Would you like to interview Cliff Richard?

in sight. To enjoy an hour of Cliff Richard's time was something I'll always be extremely grateful for.

Over the years I'd met a few people who thought they were special and others who had been quite arrogant. That was not Cliff Richard. He is such a genuine, modest and endearing person. That was a day to remember – and his office girls even made me lunch.

So far, that programme has produced the greatest ever response for a *John Hannam Meets*. I received many letters, and a competition brought in seventy 'phone calls in next to no time. We had extra people to man the lines. Cliff even asked for a tape for his family. Thanks Vic.

Like millions of others, I admired everything that Terry Waite represented and achieved. It's hard to envisage what life was like for him during his confinement as a hostage. Being blindfolded and chained must have been humiliating and unbearable to a degree we can't even begin to imagine. When given the opportunity to visit him in a Southampton bookshop I could barely wait.

Terry's a giant in every way and such a delight to be with. To discover how they set up a message tapping code system on cell pipes was quite extraordinary. Some weaker men, clearly, would not have pulled through.

Despite his ordeal, Terry Waite still maintained his sense of humour. When the guards took the blindfolds off, they showed some sympathy towards him and even smuggled in two English books for him to read, which was a serious risk to take. The first was on breast-feeding and the other a Dr Spock book on babies – and he read them both.

I've long admired songwriters and Les Reed, who wrote many hits for Tom Jones and Engelbert Humperdinck, had always been in the forefront. Les was once in the John Barry Seven, and then went on to front those spectacular Pop Proms on television.

Craig Douglas and Les had appeared in a musical, about a bandleader, at Sonning. Craig sent me a superbly produced Les Reed biography. That eventually led to a visit to Les's country house in Hampshire.

What a welcome, too. Coffee with Les and June and then the luxury of his gorgeous lounge as my mobile recording studio. Nothing was too much trouble for Les, and he loaned some of his rare albums to use on the programme.

Thankfully, he was pleased with the show and offered to help me obtain other guests. That was an offer I couldn't refuse. A few names immediately spring to mind.

A few months after visiting Les I heard a quite brilliant Radio 2 programme, hosted by Don Black, on the tenth anniversary of Matt Monro's death. I was enthralled and badly wanted to meet Don Black, Matt's former manager and a world-famous songwriter, with hits like *Walk Away, Born Free, True Grit, I'll Put You Together Again, On Days Like These* and *Love Changes Everything*.

I called Les and two days later I was in the loft when the 'phone rang and it was Don Black. Would I like to come up to London to interview him? His friend, Les Reed, had hinted that I'd rather like to.

That friendship with Les Reed was also to lead me to Lionel Bart, at home in Acton, Ron Goodwin, in the Berkshire countryside, and Tony Macaulay in breezy Brighton. All two-hour specials recorded on location.

A trip to London to meet Anthony Newley and Leslie Bricusse was not so successful. The plan was to publicise their *Scrooge* production, due in at the Mayflower, Southampton. The venue was Bromley, in Kent, and I was also offered the chance to go to London, earlier in the day, to meet Leslie Bricusse, at home. When I arrived at Leslie's wonderful city house, with all the trimmings of a millionaire, I discovered a BBC radio reporter already there, who was also going to interview him for their local station network. When she remarked how impressed she was with my recording equipment and double mike stand, I felt rather flattered. It was certainly better than her BBC supply.

Being a gentleman, I offered to let her go first. It was an offer she refused. That rather unsettled me. I hate doing interviews with other media people in the room. I was even more peeved when I noticed her taking notes during my interview with Leslie. Obviously, her homework hadn't been as thorough.

Leslie, a songwriting genius, wanted to keep his mobile 'phone on during the interview. This meant several interruptions and ruined the flow of conversation. I'm not so sure I ever used the final result.

En route to Bromley to meet Anthony Newley, which had supposedly been pre-arranged by the PR company, I dropped into Soho to interview an old Island mate, Rod Gammons, a musician, songwriter and record producer.

When I finally reached Bromley, I was told Mr Newley was too tired to see me and in fact didn't even know I was coming. Thankfully, one of my old television favourites, Stratford Johns, who played Inspector Barlow in *Z Cars* and *Softly Softly*, came to the rescue and willingly undertook an interview. Good he was, too.

There are always funny situations that stay in your memory. Caroline, who often joined me on interview assignments – which is probably how she got the desire to choose a career in costumes for television, stage and film – once came to Sandown when I was due to interview John Miller, a relation of the world famous band-leader. When she got back to the stage door, after a few minutes on the slot machines, she revealed that her dad was in the theatre interviewing Glenn Miller. That would have been a world scoop, if not a miracle! On another occasion she slightly confused one of Frankie Howerd's catch phrases, stating: "All fur knickers and no coat."

Kenny Baker, all of three foot eight, who played R2-D2 in *Star Wars*, had been live on *John Hannam Meets* on a couple of occasions, including a joint show with Jethro. I'd also interviewed him live on stage at the Sandown Pavilion. He was on the Island one Sunday and was listening to the show, and thought he'd pop in to see one of the guests. Apparently, he got to the front door of the radio station but couldn't reach the bell. We never knew he was there.

A comedy duo who should have made it to the top are the Simmons Brothers. They have been seen on some prime time television but it's their live act that takes some beating. They have strong connections with the Island and Keith met his wife here. Many years ago they were entertainers at Nodes Point, St Helens.

Keith and Alan are proud to be Water Rats and do a lot of good work for charity. Keith now writes scripts for many top pantomimes and television shows. They always appear in one of Britain's top Christmas shows.

Jethro and R2-D2, live on the same radio show.

The boys came to Southampton in December, 1994, for a star-studded panto season and invited me to the Mayflower, with my tape recorder, to meet them. In between shows they put me in a room and told me to set up my equipment and just sit there. They would do the rest. It was some line-up. Into the room, reminiscent of a doctor's surgery, came Kriss Akabusi for consultation and then in not too quick succession, which was just as well, came Lesley Joseph, John Nettles, Rosemary Ford, Jeffrey Holland and Windsor Davies. That was an hour to cherish. Lesley, completely different from her television image, was really feeling unwell but insisted on keeping our date. Millions of men would have loved to have changed places with me.

Meeting John Inman at a later Southampton pantomime was another treasured moment. He was free to record a half-hour chat. The repeats of *Are You Being Served?* are funnier than virtually all of today's excuses for TV situation comedies. John is now one of the great panto dames.

Another pantomime mission was to Guildford to meet Bill Maynard, Greengrass from *Heartbeat*. Back in the '50s Bill had been one of my comedy idols in *Great Scott It's Maynard*, with Terry Scott.

When I arrived, Bill was lying down in his dressing room. I managed to fit the microphone stand into the perfect position so he could stay just as he was. He's a lovely guy and it all worked like clockwork.

When one of the stage hands came in, Bill asked her to go shopping for him. It was just a little too late for her to leave the theatre. So I volunteered. Bill wanted a new toothbrush, tooth paste and bar of soap. He gave me a fiver and my errand was under way. When I brought back the goods and the change, he couldn't believe it. "I normally don't get any change," said Bill.

That day his agent had turned down an offer of £50,000 for him to to appear in a television commercial. He had asked for more money, on Bill's behalf. From what he told me, Bill was really not too worried, anyway. Not a star governed by money.

Whilst in his dressing room, Bill arranged for an interview with his now estranged wife, Tonia Bern-Campbell, who was in a Dartford panto. He lived in England while Tonia lived in the States. "She'll do it. Just tell her I said she would," suggested Bill. He was right, too. Interviewing the widow of Donald Campbell was a fascinating experience.

Pantomimes are great because they are an opportunity to meet stars and celebrities you would normally not come into contact with.

Britt Ekland is a film star who's been the fantasy of millions of men – and the reality of others, slightly more famous, like Peter Sellers, Rod Stewart and Ryan O'Neal. My request for an interview was readily agreed and, apparently, my letter had guaranteed I was in the lucky list. Top stars get numerous requests for interviews and some journalists are always disappointed. I know that feeling, as well.

Britt arrived late and had 'phoned to say she'd been delayed. Then I was finally ushered into her dressing room – and there she was. Or was it? There was this world-famous blonde film star, with black hair. I was somewhat bemused. Britt was obviously running late and decided to paint her finger nails throughout the interview. When she realised I didn't really want to talk much about Peter Sellers or any of her other men friends or husbands, she seemed quite relaxed. Within minutes she was on stage playing a real baddie, with frightening realism. It was just as well I didn't upset her.

Back on the Isle of Wight, where Britt had once made a movie called

Endless Night, close friends asked me what her blonde hair was like. Even my hairdresser, Tracey Squibb from Newport's Hairlines International, was dying to know about the famous Britt locks. When I revealed that Britt's hair was actually black, she, like many others, thought I was losing the plot. It was even suggested that it could have been my age playing tricks.

When my 'Girl Sunday', Jessica Snazell, came into the radio station the following week-end she had the perfect explanation. It must have been Britt's street wig – a perfect disguise.

I still insist I interviewed a black-haired Britt Ekland.

CHAPTER FOURTEEN

A BEVY OF BEAUTIES &
A LOTTERY TREBLE

Let's stay on the beauty trail. Another panto star at the Mayflower was Ann Sidney, a former Miss World. I couldn't call that interview work. Ann is still so beautiful and desirable. We quickly hit it off, and before you get any ideas, Caroline was sat behind dad. Heather can be quite clever, at times.

Ann was very friendly and even sent me a postcard from America a few months later. Back on the day England won the World Cup, in 1966, I'd seen

Ann Sidney – she still looks like a Miss World.

more of Ann Sidney than I'd bargained for. We were backstage at the Playhouse Theatre, Bournemouth, to watch the musical *Lock Up Your Daughters*, starring Craig Douglas, Bill Maynard and Ann. In those days I was still star struck and would always glance in dressing-room doors. On this occasion I saw parts of her I shouldn't have, in the mirror. I looked away as quickly as I could. Don't get perturbed. Now you can see similar sights every day of the week in the *Sun*.

Thanks to Mark Watson, from the Wayne Peak organisation, and Les Pink at Sandown's Carlton Hotel, I was able to meet Michelle Collins before she

Mr and Mrs Smith? I should be so lucky! Miss Collins and Mr Hannam at the Carlton.

opened the nearby Scruffy Jacks, on Sandown Pier. I wasn't a fan of *EastEnders* but knew all about Michelle and admired her work. Some time earlier she'd been one of Mari Wilson's Sensations.

Time was short but we made friends quickly and created an instant rapport that really worked on air. It was one of those occasions when I didn't want the interview to end. Since then, I've enjoyed her hit series like *Real Women*, one of the funniest things I've ever seen on television, particularly the last episode of the first series, and *Sunburn*.

Whilst in the Carlton reception saying goodnight to Michelle, I noticed another familiar face. It was Craig Shergold, the youngster who had success-fully recovered from cancer. He'd had millions of get-well cards, through world-wide publicity. I went back the next day to interview him. That was a real hoot.

After Michelle Collins, Koo Stark was quite a different proposition, at the Dimbola Lodge, Freshwater Bay. I was promised fifteen minutes but was lucky to get even five. It may well have been that Koo doesn't trust the media. I had to work hard to get what I did – and I didn't mention you-know-who.

On the same afternoon I also interviewed Lydia Heston, the wife of the Hollywood movie icon. That was an experience not to be missed. I had her husband in my sights. He had been here on one occasion but unfortunately was running behind schedule. Still, there was hope – as you'll find out.

Dora Bryan is always a challenge that is well worth the gamble. I first met her at the Chichester Festival Theatre. In the spring of 1998 she came to open a bridal fair at Gurnard Pines. Interviewing Dora is real seat-of-the-pants stuff. She admits to being eccentric and you can never really relax. I loved the uncer-tainty of her responses and, of course, her endless anecdotes.

The previous evening Dora and her husband, Bill Lawton, a former county cricketer and coach, had an embarrassing and costly experience. They parked their car outside of their log cabin. An hour or so later they heard a loud bump in the night, caused by their pride and joy rolling down the slope into the next cabin. The car was a write-off!

After that Saturday morning interview, Dora announced she wanted to take her new friend (me), for a morning coffee on the terrace. We had a few photographs taken together and then came a quite surprising moment. A lady from the centre's gift shop brought over an Island souvenir and presented it to me for my wife and myself, as a memento of our visit. She thought Dora and I were married. For once in my life, I would have been a toyboy. What a combi-nation that might have proved.

When Ryde Arena announced plans to present Elkie Brooks, it was agreed with the tour promoters that I would go to Basingstoke to interview her to publicise the Island gig. That seemed fine, particularly as no interviews had been allowed on her previous visit to Ryde Arena.

I arrived at Basingstoke and was told to wait for the tour manager. Apparently they had not been advised that I was coming and Elkie had a policy of no interviews whilst on tour. Would I like to go and have a cup of tea with the crew? Elkie's manager, her husband, came to find me and stated there was no way she would see me. I pleaded that it had all been arranged with the tour company.

The long wait was frustrating but Elkie took pity on me and agreed to a few minutes. I was so relieved when she walked through the door and sat down at the other end of the mike stand.

I could only get about half the time I'd planned for but had an idea, on the journey home. Whilst waiting for the Red Jet on the outward trip I had seen a blind lad waiting for the craft and helped him aboard. At Southampton I guided him on to the Central Station bus. "Are you John Hannam?" he enquired. He had recognised my voice. There and then he asked me to sign an autograph. That was not a regular occurrence.

When we arrived at the station I took him for a cup of tea and then we parted to go on different trains. With the Elkie Brooks interview proving to be shorter than planned, I subsequently invited that same young man, Simon Highsmith, to appear live on my show. He thoroughly enjoyed himself and proved quite a hit.

It was like a breath of fresh air when Pam Ayres burst on the scene, following great success on *Opportunity Knocks*. Virtually all her Island appearances have been sell-outs.

In February 1994 I went to her home, near Cirencester, to record an interview. It was an idyllic setting. When we arrived, Pam was gardening in her wellies and before long we were in her huge kitchen having a nice pot of tea. Then her children came in with muddy feet and it was like being in anyone's home. They were then asked to be quiet because of our pending radio interview – and they even managed that.

My first-ever visit to Eastbourne was to meet two people who had nothing in common – other than being in show business.

Ted Rogers, who'd long been a good friend, had suffered a few miserable years. The days of London Palladium seasons with stars like Bing Crosby, New York residences and the chart-topping *3-2-1* had long gone. Ted, like so many others, had been ripped off. On numerous occasions he'd been given poor advice and fortunes can soon bite the dust, as he found out to his cost.

Ted, a born fighter, was coming back and enjoying his panto season in Sussex. We had lunch, did a super backstage interview and then saw a matinée. It was a little different when I moved up the road to the Congress Theatre to meet international movie and stage star Topol.

That was not quite as easy. Mr Topol's personal assistant was a little over fastidious and everything had to be just so. She was worried about the time for his warm up vocal exercises. When I finally got to meet Topol he was most charming and courteous and warmed, considerably, during our interview.

Whilst reflecting on Eastbourne, Russ Conway, who lives there, comes to mind. He has always been one of my favourite showbiz characters. On one occasion Heather and I enjoyed a visit to his home. During his Island début season, in the '80s, he'd kindly opened the Godshill school fête, when my daughter was still a pupil there. He was virtually mobbed – and enjoyed every minute. What an extraordinary man, with such determination. Once in an epic week of his life he had Britain's top selling single and album, and was on the number one television show. That couldn't happen anymore. Despite having a stroke during the '60s and cancer in the '80s, he's pulled through and is still undertaking concerts well into his seventies.

Russ Conway being mobbed when opening Godshill school fête.

Another legendary British musician was trumpet star Nat Gonella, who died in 1998, at the age of 90. My father had been a keen Nat Gonella fan, who fronted his own brilliant big band during the '30s and '40s. Dad died not knowing that Nat appeared twice on my chat show. We did dedicate the first interview to his memory. The last time I ever saw Nat was on a Saturday blessed with mixed fortunes. It was actually the day of his ninetieth birthday and, unexpectedly at that time, it was to be his very last interview. A few weeks later he passed away.

Nat was great fun on that Saturday morning in Brighstone, where he was staying with local friends, John and Anna Wortham. The trumpet genius had a glint in his eye when he saw my little bit of trouble. I'd backed into John's narrow drive and was slightly off angle on the steep slope. I heard a thump and realised I'd smashed one of Anna's large earthenware pots and the back wheel of the car had gone over the edge of the raised drive. There was no way I could drive out.

The RAC were 'phoned and while we were waiting, I interviewed Nat. "Have you had a little bit of a problem, mate?" asked Nat. Perhaps my embarrassed gaze had given it away. Nat calmed me down and in the end no damage was done. The interview was accomplished, the RAC man towed me out and Anna had a new pot. Why worry? Anna also took a few pictures of Nat and me but the camera was faulty, so they didn't come out. What a day!

I talked earlier of the ill-fated 1990 Isle of Wight Pop Festival at Smallbrook. A year or two later there was another open-air event there, organised by Isle of

Wight Radio. Once again, the crowds were disappointing. There were a sprinkling of '60s and '70s bands, including Mungo Jerry, the Pretty Things and Love Affair. The latter just had the original lead singer, Steve Ellis.

The Pretty Things were fun to interview and Ray Dorset, the lead singer of Mungo Jerry, was very obliging. I wish I could say the same about Steve Ellis, from Love Affair. He was nothing less than an arrogant pig and I don't know how I managed to sit through the interview. He had no real interest, queried facts that I knew were correct and generally went out of his way to be difficult. In the end, for the first time ever, I had a go at a guest during an interview. Heather who was sat in the same room was disgusted by his attitude.

It's quite amazing. I'd met some of the greatest stars in the world and had no problems. The virtually unknown singer of a '60s pop group, who were reputed to be session men anyway, gave me such a hard time. The interview was never played. What a fantastic voice he had, too.

When '70s pop star Suzi Quatro came to the Sandown Pavilion she was tired out, having travelled from Yorkshire. The American-born rock star was noticeably unhappy at the prospect of carrying out the pre-arranged interview. I could sense her complete lack of interest as she merely went through the motions. There were just no vibes at all, however I tried. It would have been far easier if Suzi had just said she didn't want to do it. That was another interview to go through the wiping machine.

Eighties pop star Howard Jones was such a different person altogether and the chance to meet him came about through local boy Les Payne. I'd interviewed Les on many occasions and loved his attitude to life and his total infatuation with becoming a rock star. He deserved to make it and has made some fantastic records, particularly with his old group, Mainland. Les came back home for the launch of that magnificent *Isle of Wight Rock* publication, at which I was so honoured to introduce a few guests at Northwood House.

During an informal chat with Les, he revealed his friendship with Howard Jones. That was all the hint I needed. Within a week I was in Howard's Maidenhead home, doing an interview in his impressive garden studio. Howard and his wife were such genial hosts.

While I chatted to Howard, his eight-year-old son Osheen entertained Heather. He was most definitely a star in the making – and had the self-confidence to back it up. Since that kitchen showcase, he's made a film with Anthony Hopkins.

Through local friend, musician and entertainments manager David Wright, I was invited up to BBC Television Centre to meet one of TV's golden girls, Carol Smillie. The plan was for Caroline and myself to travel to the rehearsals of the Wednesday Lottery Show and interview Carol during a break. It worked to perfection. Carol, a supreme professional, was an infectious lady who made us feel so at home.

We sat through several run-throughs and realised the Lightning Seeds were going to sing their latest single, *You Showed Me*. The band were sat right near us and there was nothing to lose in asking Ian Broudie for the chance of an interview. He was most helpful and suggested I arranged it with his manager. The outcome was something of a scoop.

Also on that particular show was Grand National winner Tony Dobbin, who'd won the race a couple of days earlier. He was also willing to talk. That was a good afternoon's work – rounded off nicely by meeting another famous person, whilst waiting to interview Ian of the Lightning Seeds.

We were in a corridor when a really friendly guy in a baseball cap called out to us and asked us why we were there. We had a laugh or two and he went on his way. Then Caroline suddenly realised it was Dale Winton. When he came back a few minutes later we apologised that we had not recognised him in a baseball cap. "That's the general idea," quipped Dale.

Just as we were leaving, another very important person arrived in a breath-taking car. It was Sir David Frost. We'd really enjoyed our away-day at the BBC.

I interviewed another television celebrity much closer to home – in the Newport Guildhall, to be precise. Loyd Grossman came for an appearance at the new museum. We had a great time.

Fred Dinenage is a legend on the Island and along the South Coast – a supreme television presenter and such a joy to be with. Our paths have crossed a few times and we've made the most of it. He did a great two-hour special for *John Hannam Meets* and then turned the tables by interviewing me. That was scary. We share a similar sense of humour – and hairstyle.

One of the best theatre contacts in the South of England was Sandra Smith at the Kings, Southsea. Nothing was too much trouble for her and she possessed PR and administration skills that were much respected by both artists and the media alike. It was her perseverance that persuaded Marti Webb, starring there in *Evita*, to undertake a rare interview. Surprisingly, Marti is quite a shy person.

I arrived on time, only to be told that Marti would be late. There had been a party the previous night and she was walking to the theatre. Time

Only the hairlines have changed in thirty years. Fred Dinenage put me in the hot seat.

was running short before curtain-up for the Wednesday matinée. We only started talking a few minutes away from the advertised opening time of the show. Marti seemed unconcerned and said we could keep going.

If was only after the performance that I discovered the show had been put back, so we were able to finish comfortably. On the hovercraft ride home people asked if it was me who'd been doing the important interview. It had been announced in the theatre.

Sandra Smith came up trumps with so many panto stars, and others she arranged included John Altman, who played Nick Cotton in *EastEnders*; Harry Worth; Marius Goring, another Island-born actor; Hayley Mills; Tony Scannell, who played Ted Roach in *The Bill*, and Jenny Seagrove.

When Gerry Marsden, one of the most durable of the '60s pop stars, came to Sandown it took more than a little persuasion to get him to talk. Eventually he promised just a few minutes. Over the past thirty years I'd got to know virtually all the major '60s stars as good friends or acquaintances. These included Joe Brown, Cliff Bennett, Jet Harris, Marty Wilde, Dave Berry, still such a charismatic performer, the Searchers, the Merseybeats and John Leyton. With regard to Gerry Marsden, I hardly knew him at all.

During our taped conversation he stressed how close friends we were and it was always nice to come to the Isle of Wight to see old mates like me. After the broadcast many people remarked they hadn't realised Gerry and I were such good buddies – nor had I.

Gerry is a fantastic performer. I've never seen him do a poor show. He just continues to turn it on. One or two of his contemporaries just go through he motions.

CHAPTER FIFTEEN

A LATE NIGHT IN DODDYLAND

I TRIED VERY hard to tempt Ken Dodd to the Isle of Wight. He even made a public promise to appear at Sandown. Now, of course, it's too late. It was in 1996 that Heather and I took Mimi Law, an old mate of Doddy's, to meet him in Hunstanton. Ken had agreed to an interview and we were due to meet him in his secluded hotel. When we arrived we were met by his girlfriend, Annie, who advised us that Ken was busy but would join us for afternoon tea.

Ken bounded into the room and it was as if we'd known him all our lives – obviously Mimi had. That tea party was delightfully manic. Eventually Ken and I slipped off to a quiet room for our hour-long chat. That was short by his standards.

Earlier we'd been to the Princess Theatre, Hunstanton, only to discover that the show had been long sold out. Had Ken got us tickets? No-one knew, although three were booked in his name.

After the interview, Annie arranged to

With Doddy at Hunstanton.

meet us in the theatre foyer. The three tickets were ours. I was just about to pay at the box-office when Annie rushed through and said "These are on Ken".

We'd heard the rumours that if you go to a Ken Dodd concert you need to take a flask and sandwiches. It started at 7.30 p.m. and was still going 12.15 a.m. In all, Ken did four hours of his material and had two support acts. At 11.30 he told the audience: "All around Hunstanton baby-sitters are looking out of the windows wondering where the parents are. You won't be home yet."

There was an invite to Doddy's dressing room. He started again, with another hour-long session. All new gags and anecdotes. We finally crept into our sea-front guest house around 2 a.m. We had to ask Ken if we could go, as we had an early start that same morning. It must have been daylight before he left that theatre.

Through Mimi and Billy, we'd got to know Deryck Guyler and his super wife Paddy. Whenever Derry came to their house, we got an invite. Being in his company was so invigorating. On a Saturday night, in late 1990, I picked Deryck up for a live *John Hannam Meets*. The trip from Ryde to Newport was

was uneventful, other than his splendid company. On the way back there was an amazing storm. We had to drive through torrents of rain and it was quite a horrendous journey. After dropping Derry back at Ryde, we drove home through Sandown and Lake (what an appropriate name), where manhole covers were floating in the roads. It was touch and go whether Caroline, Sean and I could get back to Godshill, with the extent of the flooding near Whitely Bank.

That Ken Dodd experience has set me thinking about other famous stars who I've been so privileged to meet, for varying reasons.

Vince Hill was such an inspiration to Heather and I. We had encountered problems in starting a family. Over several years we'd both had tests. Heather had been to University College Hospital, London, and I'd been locally. All to no avail – yet there was always hope. We were fans of Vince Hill and often waited behind, after his string of Sandown Pavilion shows, in the late '60s, to have a chat and get records signed. I was not writing regular columns or broadcasting at that time.

Frisby Dyke, Corky, Norman Potter, The Washboard King – and a few floating manhole covers. A wet Saturday night drive with Deryck Guyler.

Vince and his wife Ann had recently been blessed with their first child, Atholl. One of our conversations with Vince got around to talking about Atholl, who was on one of his album covers. Then he disclosed they had been trying for fourteen years to start a family. For us it had been around ten years, by that time. Vince and

With Vince Hill, twenty-five years after his advice paid off.

92

Ann's story was a great source of inspiration for us – and so it proved. In the end we waited eleven years for Sean. Now we know Vince as a good friend and often remind him of that story.

In the '70s, during a family holiday in Devon, I went to interview Moira Anderson at the Princess Theatre, Torquay. This had been arranged through a mutual friend. Larry Grayson was topping the bill. I'd been told he was unlikely to do an interview – so I didn't try. As I went to find Moira's dressing room, I met Larry on the stairs. He had no idea who I was or what I was doing there, but was very welcoming and friendly. Had my advisers been wrong? It was too late to find out then.

However, I did find out many years later, when he came for an epic summer at Sandown. We met for an interview in the Cliff Tops Hotel. Larry was such a great guy and what a sense of fun. He was so popular that he couldn't go out shopping or just for a walk. He was continually mobbed. He did try to go into a Regent Street shop but was immediately recognised and had to withdraw quickly.

That was one of his major disappointments, but he realised it was all part of being such a popular figure. He loved his public. After all, he'd waited over thirty years to become a major name.

During that summer, Sandown Pavilion Theatre manager Jan Fletcher renewed her friendship with Larry Grayson. They had been in shows together, when Larry was unknown.

As happy as Larry at the Sandown Pavilion, 1982 – then 'Slack Alice' arrived.

93

It's all too easy for young people to laugh off Max Bygraves, without knowing his true pedigree. When I was growing up he was probably the greatest star in Britain and his catch phrases like 'big head' and 'it's a good idea son' were on everyone's lips. Later he unearthed others like 'big money' on *Family Fortunes*, and, of course, 'I wanna tell you a story'.

I was thrilled to interview Max on a couple of occasions and was completely shocked to find he actually had listened to my programme, in Bournemouth. He's such an interesting character and really has done it all. He's made movies, starred at every major British theatre, hosted TV shows, starred in his own and sold millions of albums. When Max came to Warner's Norton Grange, for a special week-end cabaret, as he walked on stage the whole audience stood up and cheered. The hallmark of real fame. He flew in and out of Yarmouth by helicopter.

What a good idea, son! When Max Bygraves walked on stage, the whole audience stood and cheered. A real 'staralongamax'.

Charlie Williams is also a tonic. When he did seasons at Sandown you could see him on the front, during the day, selling the show to the punters. His beautiful wife revealed a great story on *John Hannam Meets*. They were staying in a huge hotel when the fire alarm went off. At the time she was in the bath. Charlie left her to it and ran for the fire exit. I'm not so sure she's forgiven him for that.

On another live visit to the studio I arranged to pick him up, from personal friends in Brading, at around 12.15 p.m., in readiness for the 1 o'clock show. The only problem was I couldn't find him. After almost twenty minutes of circumnavigating Brading, I noticed him stood on a wall in The Mall. That was a little too tight for comfort. We only just made it.

Someone else who left it a little late was Danny Williams. He's such a cool guy and offered to come down from London, just to do my radio show. Dan was due to start the show at 6 p.m. It was after the time slot had been changed. Ron Shepperd was going to pick him up from the 4.20 catamaran. It was the day after the clocks should have been put forward. Dan had forgotten, which was completely out of character. This meant he missed the ferry and arrived just as I was introducing the show. There was a certain hesitancy in my intro, as I was not sure if he'd made it. All of a sudden the studio hosts for the day, my postman Tony Smith and his wife Ann, signalled the thumbs up sign. I was just about to change the running order and start with a taped interview with Fern Britton, I'd recently recorded at Olympia, due for the second hour of the show.

I'll never forget Jasper Carrot's first-ever Island appearance. It was a riot of fun. He got quite the wrong impression of Island life, for one brief moment. He noticed the super houses in Fishbourne Lane and thought the the rest of us were just as wealthy. On stage he did joke about those properties with their 'servants'.

When he came back, with Phil Cool, it was a sensational night. Phil, who'd always turned down the star television chat show hosts like Michael Parkinson and Terry Wogan, would always come on mine. That night I gave them a few local tips to get a laugh or two. This also worked a little later on for Jo Brand – and Morris Barton didn't mind at all. Our former Council leader has always been welcome on my radio or television shows.

One of my great pleasures is meeting true self-made men. Fred Pontin was the perfect example. He endured really hard times and took a gamble. He also kept a tight personal reign on his holiday centres, including our own Little Canada. It seemed fitting that our interview was at the Farringford, one of his favourite places. He was also the owner.

On an Easter week-end at the Farringford I also caught up with songwriter, agent and record producer Bunny Lewis. What a fantastic story he had to tell. He wrote *Cara Mia* for David Whitfield and, years later, *Girl Of My Best Friend* for Elvis. He also had an admirable war record. I have so much time for these people.

When I was in my teens, watching *Oh Boy!* was a must – not only for Marty and Cliff but for my favourite Vernon Girl, Maggie Stredder, the one with the glasses. I must admit, I did have a thing for ladies in glasses. I'm not so sure that's ever changed. Getting to know Maggie and tracing her life, which included the Ladybirds, the girl singing trio who appeared on all the hit TV shows, including Benny Hill's, was such a delight. I was even invited to her wedding.

The year of 1998 culminated in a sort of Royal Appointment. More on that, later. It was to prove an unforgettable twelve months. I had more time to pursue my journalistic career and the chance to host my own television series was an added bonus.

There was an early shock with the death of a really close friend, Wally Malston, one of Britain's top television script writers. He'd begun by writing gang shows for the Cowes scouts. En route to interviewing Cliff Michelmore, near Petersfield, we'd called in to see Wally at the Fleet Hospice. We spent an hour in his company and realised just how poorly he was. Stars like Bruce Forsyth and Ted Rogers had been among his previous visitors. Bruce had been away on holiday in South America and had virtually gone straight from the airport to the hospital.

It was a sad occasion. Wally was unable to speak, but we left knowing in our hearts that he was aware we were there. Later that day he passed away.

At his Aldershot funeral there was a host of entertainers, top comedy writers and television producers. No-one wanted it to be a sad occasion. Wally wouldn't have wanted that. A few of his local Island pals like Brian Munro, Mike Bizzill and Ian Moody also made the journey.

The service began as any other and then the vicar introduced Bruce Forsyth, who would say a few words. Bruce was quite brilliant. He virtually gave a stand-up routine on his long association with Wally. Thankfully, everyone laughed. That send-off could have been scripted by Wally himself. Everyone remembered him with a smile .

After the service, at the Aldershot Crematorium, I was introduced to Bruce. He remarked: "I know your name, John. Didn't you and I do an interview, set up by Wally?"

To put you in the picture, Wally had tried to arrange it a year or two earlier but Bruce's commitments would not permit it. There was a 'phone interview offered but I didn't want that. It had been in the pending tray.

In reply to Bruce's question, I had to say we'd never actually ever got together. Knowing how much Wally wanted this interview, I found myself saying to Bruce how nice it would be to do a programme in memory of our

Brucie and Johnny – that's his house, not mine.

mutual friend. Bruce liked the idea and suggested I came up to his home in a couple of months time. Would I ring him in a few weeks?

When I 'phoned at the pre-arranged time, Bruce was very keen to follow up the idea and suggested a date. Later he 'phoned back, a call taken by Sean, much to his delight, as I was out. The message hinted there could now be a problem. Something special was due to happen over that very week-end. Our date was for Monday morning, June 15, at his Wentworth home. Could I perhaps ring him the night before? It was all rather mysterious.

The secret was revealed on the Saturday morning. It was Bruce Forsyth, OBE. When I rang him at home on the Sunday night, as arranged, he said the next day's interview was still on, despite all the excitement. Mine was just beginning. I congratulated him, of course.

Brucie was a genial host. I spent a couple of hours in his fantastic house. We had both kept our promise to Wally. I found Bruce such a modest and unassuming character. Unfortunately his wife, Wilnelia, was away for a few days. In her absence, the house-keeper made me feel very welcome.

I did have one anxious moment. I set-up in Bruce's luxurious lounge and my two mike stands were stood very close to a glass table full of beautiful ornaments. I just prayed the stands wouldn't topple over.

Another truly great professional is Bob Monkhouse. I've met him numerous times and have never failed to be impressed. During the final week

of his Sandown summer season I saw every show and he changed his material every night. When Bob once came later to appear at the Ryde Theatre we did an interview, recorded live, in August, which was played in November. It was recorded in Isle of Wight Radio's Studio B. Bob was so clever and never put a foot wrong.

His early love for showbusiness, and comedians in particular, had been initiated here on the Island, when he watched summer season shows with names like Arthur Askey, at Shanklin in 1936, and Eric Barker, the following year at Sandown.

Bob had been the first comedian that Wally Malston had ever written material for. During one of Bob's visits, I got the two of them together for a newspaper story.

Bob Monkhouse and Wally Malston
– both comedy geniuses.

Jimmy Cricket was another top name who summered at Sandown. As a family, we hit it off with Jimmy and Maud and their children. One Sunday, on Jim's day off, we decided to take all our youngsters to Rookley Country Park. Jimmy rolled up at our house in his brand new Ford Granada and suggested we all went in that, as it was bigger than my Escort.

With everyone settled in this glistening new car, it wouldn't start. Jimmy had not put any petrol in. We had to borrow a can from my neighbour, Dave Miles, who was hugely amused and who – judging by his antics – was also a Jimmy Cricket fan. Eventually we made Rookley and Jimmy locked up the car. After walking a few hundred yards Maud missed their youngest son. Jimmy had locked him in the car by accident.

On a later visit to see his Island pal, local *Some Mothers Do 'Ave 'Em* writer Raymond Allen, Jimmy boarded the dotto train and was invited to sit with the driver. An embarrassed Ray tried to look the other way, seating himself further down the train.

On an early Saturday night of my radio show, I arranged to pick up Jimmy on the way to the studio. When I arrived at Puckpool no-one knew where he was. There wasn't long before we were due on air. I 'phoned the station to explain the problem, and had quite a shock. Jimmy Cricket answered my call.

CHAPTER SIXTEEN

SIR EDWARD & THE BEST MAN

BACK TO the year of 1998. With the idea of a guest for the start of Cowes Week, I contacted Sir Edward Heath's office and asked if he would be available to do an interview. Sir Edward liked the idea and I was invited to Cathedral Close, Salisbury, to meet him. So far, so good.

I arrived in plenty of time and wandered around the cathedral. When I finally rang the bell at the entrance to the house, a police officer came from nowhere and demanded my ID. I had no idea ex-Prime Ministers were still always guarded. All I had was my tape recorder, guest book and train and ferry tickets. It was looking a little hairy but Sir Edward's personal assistant was waving from the front door. As soon as I mentioned her name, the gate was opened.

In the end, after several changes of plan, Sir Edward chose the garden for an outdoor location. How had I cracked this? I couldn't believe it. An ex-Prime Minister. My mum would never believe it.

That year Isle of Wight Radio also went to FM. I was asked if I had any suggestions for a star to attend our open day, on Sunday March 29. I knew Tom O'Connor was at Warner's Bembridge Coast, the night before, and he stayed over just to appear at the open day and be a live guest on my lunch-time show. Everyone at the station and all the public were so impressed by Tom's appearance, professionalism and manner. He wasn't acting. That is Tom O'Connor, one of the great gentlemen of the business. He is still the world record holder for hosting TV game shows. On the way in we stopped off for morning coffee at the Round House Tea Rooms, Fairlee, and Andy and Pam were thrilled to bits. So were the customers. Tom just chatted like an old friend to all of them. His wife, Pat, is another gem.

When I received a press release from Meridian inviting me to a première of

Tom O'Connor – always a gent.

Edward Windsor's *Crown and Country*, at Petworth House, I cheekily faxed back a request for a personal face-to-face interview. Incredibly, it was on.

We had a couple of days in Eastbourne and then headed for Sussex. A quiet walk around the grounds put me in a perfect mood. Heather and I were ushered into the press room with about a dozen other media people. All of a sudden Prince Edward just walked in and sat amongst us.

When the time came for the interview Meridian's chief press officer had found us a peaceful place. It was actually a mock by-gone kitchen of an old country house. No sooner had I set up when in walked Edward. The body-guard gave us some space and remained outside. Apparently, he was now running late and the promised ten minutes was in question. He'd over-run with Meridian's Peter Henley.

I did my acting bit and felt very confident, and Edward was enjoying our chat. Unbeknown to me, at the time, they were giving Heather the wind-up sign after two or three minutes. Heather ignored the sign – well, she had been brought up the right way. In any case, she couldn't catch my eye. When the ten minutes were up I ended the conversation. Nothing was said. Another five minutes and I might have ended up in the Tower. As we left, so did Edward and his detective. We waved goodbye and walked half a mile to our diesel Mondeo. He was chauffeured to London in something rather more posh. It was our first meeting with a Royal – and we were impressed. *John Hannam Meets*, by Royal Appointment. I still can't believe it.

At last – By Royal Appointment.
(Picture by kind permission of Meridian Television.)

Guitarists have always been high on my priority list. Other than meeting Vic Flick, the Bond twang star, I was also lucky enough to meet my original idol, Duane Eddy, who was touring with the Everly Brothers. The show's compère, Dave Lee, a very funny jumbo-size comedian, took me backstage. In 1998 I also caught up with two more, Bert Weedon and Big Jim Sullivan. Bert, whom I'd interviewed several times for newspapers, finally did a radio spot. Big Jim, once of the Krew-Kats, played those superb riffs on Dave Berry's *The Crying Game* and on many of Tom Jones' hits. I interviewed him in the kitchen of a Southsea pub. That broadcast had plenty of sound effects.

Going to Chichester Festival Theatre is always a great thrill and over the years I'd met Dora Bryan, Bob Grant and Emilia Fox there. Now it was the turn of Simon Callow, who is a great admirer of the Isle of Wight. He loves the Seaview Hotel. I was asked to arrive near the end of the day's rehearsals. Their press officer, Tracey Shaw, had taken me into a delightfully relaxing office and provided refreshments. Apparently Simon was still working on his portrayal of Faust. When an hour had passed I became a little concerned – and so did the Chichester office. Simon had gone off to his digs and completely forgotten. Rumour suggested he may have gone for a walk. A message was left on his hotel answerphone, in the hope he'd return in time. There was a hint that he might not want to come back.

Simon was eventually found and came back to apologise profusely. He willingly gave me all the time I required. He's enjoyed such a varied career. It seems a pity that some only know him for playing Gareth in *Four Weddings and a Funeral*. Simon's both an acting genius and a director. He was marvellous as Mr Micawber in a television adaptation of *David Copperfield*.

Another 'first' came in the summer of '98. I actually flew to interview a guest. This made me a little apprehensive, having had a few problems with Menière's disease, which affects the inner ear.

The subject was Gilbert O'Sullivan. I'd suggested to Peter Brennen that he booked the '70s star into the Sandown Pavilion. Isle of Wight Theatres were not booking any name acts at that time. When the idea of an interview was mooted, it was pointed out that Gilbert would not undertake any on tour. His management suggested he would only talk to journalists beforehand. I would need to fly to Jersey to do this. Were they bluffing? I knew Gilbert did so few in-person interviews. When I agreed to fly out, they responded positively and fixed an exclusive chat in his Channel Islands millionaire's hideaway.

I dosed myself up with tablets and flew from Southampton to Jersey. Gilbert's brother, Kevin, had made all the arrangements and even picked me up from the airport and took me to my hotel. He promised to come back later for a drink and chat – and he did. The next morning he picked me up and we drove to Gilbert's luxury residence.

The singer/songwriter was at his happiest in his writing room, complete with a piano. We did the interview there. In the next room were thousands of LP's. What a marvellous sight.

Gilbert's lovely wife made me lunch on the patio and I could ask for no more. It was perfect Channel Islands hospitality. Then Kevin whisked me back to the airport, after a short island tour.

Flying has never been one of my favourite pastimes and getting through the customs at Southampton was an added irritation. Not content with searching all my equipment, they insisted on taking out the DAT tape machine, and even wanted to plug it in and try it, microphones and everything else that was in the equipment bag. I'd always thought I had an honest face. Perhaps my pre-flight nerves were taken as something else.

Gilbert assured me it wouldn't happen on the return trip. He was proved wrong.

There was great end to the Jersey connection. Whilst there, Gilbert told me he had once boxed on the Isle of Wight, for the Swindon British Railways club, and lost. By the time he appeared at Sandown, a week or two after the interview, with the help of Ron Jones, from the Cowes Medina ABC, I'd tracked down his local opponent from that fight, who turned out to be Newport postman Terry Sedman.

Getting the two of them rematched in a Pavilion dressing room was an unexpected bonus. Gilbert appreciated the efforts we'd made to track down his old opponent. "I think he might have won a return fight," admitted Terry. Gilbert had worn extremely well and there was not a mark on him. Terry and I both put in a bid for his hair.

Like millions of football fans I marvelled at the skills of George Best. When he took to the road, in the company of Rodney Marsh, their roadshow came to Ryde Theatre. Also on the show was Mike Osman. The morning after their gig, George and Rodney agreed to appear on my radio show. I was invited to Swainston Manor to join them for breakfast. It was just the three of

What a priceless line-up!

Marsh (QPR and England),

Best (Parkhurst Reserves),

Best (Manchester United and Northern Ireland).

us plus George's stunning girlfriend of that time, Mary. To make sure there were no problems I drove them to the studio to pre-record a spot. They were off to the mainland for a charity cricket match in the afternoon.

Driving along Forest Road it was hard to believe that George and Rodney were actually sat in my car. They were true football legends. With George's reputation of not turning up, I suggested we pretended, on air, that he'd gone absent without leave. George readily agreed. It worked to perfection and finally a famous voice was heard pleading: "Don't take the mick, I'm here."

After the recording, which was broadcast three hours later, Tony Best was waiting outside to meet George Best. I knew that would prove to be one of the great moments of Tony's life. They were photographed together. What a souvenir.

Just a year or two later Tony died, while playing indoor cricket on a Sunday morning. Such a great character with a heart of gold. Tony loved raising money for local charities.

Back in 1990 Tony and his life-long mate, Mike 'Nobby' Nobbs, a natural double act, were due to come in live on the radio, to support Edwin Starr, who was at Bogey's later that night. Tony and Nobby began their spot at 9 p.m. Edwin was expected before 9.30. In the end he never turned up, and the two of them kept going for an hour – with a little refereeing from me.

Meeting sports stars has always been a thrill for me, particularly in the days before money ruined so many sports and personalities. Names like Roger Hunt, Terry Paine, John Snow, Derek Underwood, Gordon Greenidge, David Gower and Geoff Capes were perfect ambassadors for their sport. Then there was John Conteh, Trevor Brooking, Matt Le Tissier, Alan Knight, Jimmy Dickinson, Sharron Davies, Ray Reardon, Terry Griffiths and Robin Smith.

During my years on the *Post*, I also wrote a Sports Personality column, similar to my current *County Press* Sportrait. Meeting so many wonderful Island sports people was a real privilege. Many of them have given me enormous pleasure, on and off the field.

I still treasure a compliment from Arthur Lowe. When he did a summer season at the Shanklin Theatre, I arrived for an interview and knocked on his dressing room door: "Come in, I'm just washing my hair. I'll only be a couple of minutes," quipped Arthur. Keith Newbery, the *Post's* founding editor, saw Arthur in a Ryde car park and introduced himself. Keith was a great fan of *Dad's Army*. Apparently, my name came up in conversation. "He's doing a good job," said Arthur, in that Captain Mainwaring style.

When Arthur's son, Stephen, wrote a biography on his late father, I was most touched when he contacted me and used one of my articles in the book. Arthur had a boat moored on the Medina, near the Folly Inn, and was a good sailor. Small boats have no real fascination for me, though, I have to confess.

On one occasion Roger Walker, one of Britain's best-known television faces, brought his boat into Cowes for a short break. Our interview was going to be aboard, off Spencer's Wharf. I arrived at Medina Road, Cowes, to find it was about the fourth boat out in the river. So there was I, carrying my equipment bag and microphone stand across four decks of rocking boats. Roger thought it all highly amusing.

We settled into the boat and I set up the gear. The gentle rocking was beginning to make me feel slightly off balance. Then to my horror, the battery on the tape recorder was not working. Perhaps, I was lucky – but don't tell Roger. There was no mains power available. This meant a hasty call to my brother-in-law, at Northwood, to see whether we could use their lounge as a makeshift studio. They were quite chuffed. After all, it's not every day you get Bunny from *Eldorado* in your front room. Since then Roger has starred in ITV's medics series, *Picking Up The Pieces*. A couple of days after the night Roger appeared in their bungalow, Peter and Diane excitedly rang us up. They had just seen him on *The Bill*.

Peter Eames, that same relation, had previously set me up an interview with Tony Adams, Adam Chance from *Crossroads*, also on the River Medina but further up stream. This proved another enjoyable adventure.

Tony, whom I've got to know well since then, even rang up from the *Crossroads* studio to thank me for the *Post* article. I enjoyed his company and he's been on my radio show several times. I saw him once being completely mobbed in the old International Stores at Cowes.

Jazz musicians are a special breed. Make no mistake about that, and most can drink more in a night than I can manage in a year. They seem to thrive on it and play even better, the more they consume. My initial love for jazz goes back to the trad boom of the late '50s and early '60s, when many of the top bands of that time came to the Island. Jazz nights at the Winter Gardens, Ventnor, always sold out and local folk-lore suggests that well over a thousand people squeezed into the venue to watch the Temperence Seven. With new fire regulations, that just couldn't happen any more.

In that chart-topping band was trumpeter Cephas Howard, who until quite recently owned the delightful Barn, at Arreton. I do enjoy his company – although our first planned interview session was a total disaster. He certainly wasn't my flavour of the week. After much gentle persuasion I'd finally talked Cephas into being a *Stage Talk* guest. At that time he was living on Shanklin Esplanade. On the arranged evening I arrived at his house to find a message pinned to the door. It read: "Dear Mr Hannam, I've changed my mind and don't want to do the interview. Sorry about that."

I was not impressed and went off Cephas for some time. It meant getting another guest at very short notice.

Many years later Cephas didn't need to be asked twice to appear on *John Hannam Meets*. I never hold grudges. At this time he'd just bought the Barn and the free publicity would prove useful. I also had a high regard for his son, Cephas junior, who was a quite brilliant local athlete. Even then, old man Cephas was reluctant to talk about the glory days of the Temps. It took some prising out of him.

CHAPTER SEVENTEEN

TREVOR MAKES IT A DOUBLE

GEORGE MELLY is always prepared to talk. The first time I met him, at Newport's Medina Theatre, I was unusually apprehensive. Had his reputation been over-exaggerated? It certainly had. He was most agreeable and great fun. It was to be even better a few years later.

George had been booked for a lecture at the Quay Arts Centre and it was anticipated he would talk for an hour. They obviously didn't know George Melly. I must have gone back about three times to pick him up. We had a late night interview date at the Seaview Hotel. I was to be his taxi service.

He was being courted by his newly acquired local fan club, who, obviously, gloried at being in his company – and who could blame them. Big-time George eventually took pity on his patient driver and we headed for Seaview. That was a journey and a half, as the well-lubricated George revealed some fascinating stories – not all of them suitable for broadcasting. It was almost midnight before we began our recording and George had a double whisky to put him in the perfect mood.

Many radio interviewers edit their tapes, for varying reasons. I've always tried to refrain from this policy and broadcast a chat as recorded – warts and all. I won't even cut out the gaps, if the guest is a slow talker. Others like to ponder before answering. We did have a slight problem with George – well, eleven to be quite honest. After about ten minutes of fascinating conversation, George sneezed eleven times in under two minutes. It was as if he'd taken pepper with his whisky.

It proved a headache for my clever producer, Tom Stroud, who managed a touch of the Paul Daniels and made ten disappear, without losing any words of the conversation. The only other time we had a real problem was when Ken Dodd was troubled by a tickling cough – instead of a tickling stick.

Back in the '70s Acker Bilk could have had his easiest darts match ever. It was at the Ponda Rosa and I'd just finished a chat with the genial jazzer. He said to Heather: "Do you play darts missus?" She'd never played in her life and I was not much better. He found other challengers.

The last time I met Acker Bilk was at Warner's Bembridge Coast Hotel, during their massive rebuilding programme. Acker, who doesn't walk too far these days, suggested the backstage area for the interview but it was too noisy. Nick, the entertainment's manager, gave us a key to a spare chalet and, eventually, I managed to persuade Acker into leaving the building and walking over what looked like a bomb site, owing to the contractors' efforts. It was a little further than Mr Bilk imagined.

When we finally arrived at the chalet Acker came up with the words I didn't want to hear. "What do you want, about ten minutes?" I must have looked disappointed and he sensed it and remarked: "You want a bit longer, don't you?" Following my confirmation he sent for a bottle of wine. Thirty minutes later he'd just stopped talking.

In the spare chalet were a few odd clothes scattered around the room. There were also one or two other items that Acker suggested we didn't touch – not even with gloves on. Later we found out they'd given us the wrong key. It was a holidaymaker's chalet and the occupants were out. It was just as well they didn't come back!

I love jazz and big band musicians – they have so many stories. Jack Parnell, Kenny Baker, Ken Mackintosh, Terry Lightfoot, Kenny Ball and Chris Barber are a few that spring to mind.

In late 1997 I was thrilled to receive a trophy from Jack Janzen at the Towers Hotel, Ventnor, who does a lot to promote live jazz here on the Island. It was for my small contribution in interviewing local and famous musicians. Such a nice gesture.

Being an Islander, having been born in East Cowes, back in 194? – well, a few years ago – I've always enjoyed talking to local people, from all walks of life. There are so many fascinating characters who live here.

On *John Hannam Meets* we discovered many quite amazing Islanders. They are too numerous to all get a mention here. The name of Sylvia Jones conjures up life on the Military Road. Sylv was originally suggested by David Hollis from the Brighstone Spar Stores. What a shrewd talent scout he turned out to be. Sylvia's first appearance on the show, on March 27, 1994, jammed the telephone lines. This rivalled the Cliff Richard interview for popularity. An amazing feat. She's been back on several occasions. Her local stories are uniquely told.

Since that media début both national radio and TV spots have followed. Sylvia once rang me up to ask if I minded if she went on Radio 4.

Another marvellous local rustic was given his live radio début on *John Hannam Meets*, following a couple of comments to the station's 'phone-in show. It was Havenstreet's Fred Price. He proved so popular that we made a tape in aid of the Earl Mountbatten Hospice and sold 350 copies. It was the Island's top-selling Christmas album. Not bad for a lovely old Islander telling stories about "girt plats" and other delights.

Fred Price – a top selling cassette for the Earl Mountbatten Hospice.

Other gems have included John Hayward, Jack Plucknett, Dave Woodford, Sid West, Fred Hollis, Blodwen Ward, Den Phillips, Tony Cobbett, Pat Fergusson, Pam Bateman – a blind lady who was up to all kinds of tricks for charity, including tempting me into a small aeroplane – Henry Adams, Neil Shutler, Ted Satherley, the much-missed Roy Harris, one of the nicest people I ever met, and Duncan Pryde, who was such fun. Please don't feel offended if you've been left out. All of my locals have been great entertainment and I'm sorry I can't relate all their stories here. They could fill another book. That's an idea!

Tempting Lord Ross, the Island's late Liberal MP, to a live chat show was another personal milestone. I've never been affiliated to or a member of any political party, so local politicians can trust me. I rated Steve Ross both as a man and politician. He had the Island at heart and was not imported to try and win a cheap seat. He related some wonderful stories and of his utter surprise at beating the late Mark Woodnutt to take the Island seat. His wife had said, only a few days before the election: "What if you win?" To which Steve replied: "That won't happen." That was one thing he did get wrong. He was also very popular on the local cricket circuit.

On one memorable show we had three young Island people, Eloise Fox, Philip Chandler and Hayley Price, all of whom benefited from a Dream Flight trip to Florida. Their excitement and ability to overcome their serious health problems was a real eye-opener. Sadly, only a few years later, brave Eloise died, after putting up such an admirable fight for life.

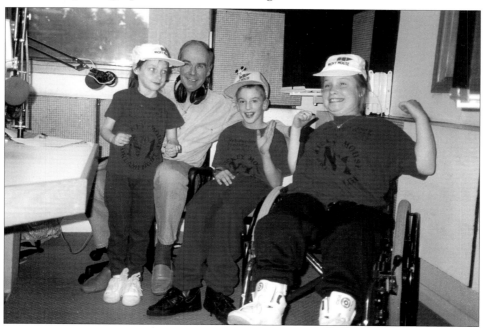

The Dream Flight kids – Eloise Fox, Philip Chandler and Hayley Price.

Among the other youngsters tempted on to the show were Luke Shaw and Danny McLaughlin. They both had health problems and were helped by listeners' donations and interest. The REACT charity, lovingly run by Brian and Rosemary Brake, was one of the local organisations which appreciated the exposure and help the programme gave them. Their gratitude is ample reward.

Sometimes unique stories just come your way. Daphne Wallis, from Sandown, came live on air the day after she met her long-lost daughter, Caroline, who'd been given away at birth, for the very first time. They both enjoyed the experience and so did the thousands of listeners.

When Steve and Ann Turner brought in their minute baby, born at just 1 lb 6 ozs, she even gurgled on air. It was a magical experience. Even I got a chance to hold Megan May. Her life was touch and go for some while. What a heart-warming story they had. There have been many others and they didn't all have such happy endings.

The death of the Island's greatest rock singer of all time, Graham Betchley, brought sadness to his many fans and friends. To give him the send-off his life and talents deserved, there was a celebration of his life at the Ryde Arena, with many of his music pals. Before then, we'd had a special tribute show on *John Hannam Meets*. The programme was packaged as a cassette, due to the generosity of Isle of Wight Radio and others, and sold to raise funds for the Earl Mountbatten Hospice, which had been so kind to Graham as well as everyone else who spends time there. We sold a thousand tapes. I watched Graham in his first-ever band, the Invaders, and loved his voice. He should have become a major British rock 'n' roll star. Deep down, he was happy here with his family and singing for friends – and he had thousands of them.

Sunday December 1, 1991, may not have seemed particularly historic at the time. There was lots to celebrate as Ryde playwright, film director, musician and great orator Anthony Minghella came in live. What a *John Hannam Meets* that was, and Anthony was in cracking form. This was the first of several visits.

Later, of course, he was to earn world acclaim for winning nine Hollywood Oscars for *The English Patient*. Many of the South of England's media had finally cottoned on to his talent. Some of us over here had long been aware of that fact. Journalists like Keith Newbery and Mike Merritt had followed his entire career with much real pleasure.

On his show début, Heather was sat next to Eddie, Anthony's father, as studio guests. Eddie whispered to her: "He hasn't mentioned my ice cream enough." Years later, of course, in Hollywood, he told the whole world about dad's ice cream.

Another Ryde writer, Raymond Allen, has always been a source of rich entertainment. He wrote *Some Mothers Do 'Ave 'Em*, as previously mentioned, but is a most under-rated speaker. Ray gets himself into such a state but is in fact a natural. We've made one or two television programmes together and he was quite brilliant. His stories about the early days of *Some Mothers* are true classics.

When Ray Alan starred in the 1988 summer season at the Shanklin Theatre, I arranged for Raymond Allen to go along and meet him. They had both been mistaken for one another. Ray is also a writer but Raymond would have problems with Lord Charles.

Ray Alan and Raymond Allen – who have both been mistaken for one another. "They are just two silly asses with the same name. What do you expect?" said their monocled friend.

Alverstone's poet Mary Ralph made her live début on *John Hannam Meets* and has since been on Radio Solent and local television. Mary has visibly blossomed and is now an accomplished performer. I must say she was very thrilled when I arranged for her to met her idol, Pam Ayres.

One of the lifers in Albany Prison invited me inside, with the help of deputy governor Bill Preston, to watch their Chequered Pasts Theatre Company's shows. Superb they were, too. Didn't I take some friendly banter from the inmates. Later, thanks to the Home Office, I was invited back to record a special show, with staff and residents.

When Apse Heath's Hilda Moore was a hundred she came in to do a live radio spot. She remembered seeing the first cars and even one of the first aeroplanes to land on the Island. Another special guest was Bembridge's Alice Lovely, who'd sailed on the first and last voyages of the P&O liner *Canberra*.

The September 1, 1996, edition of *John Hannam Meets* had an unusual twist. My guest was John Hannam. No I didn't talk to myself. It was Newport-born John, a second cousin, home from Australia. He'd emigrated there back in the '60s.

Whilst writing this book, in early 1999, stories just kept flooding in. More and more of my invitations are accepted by famous and local people.

My visits to London have became more frequent in recent times. On one of the earlier ones everything fell into plan, just at the last moment. I'd arranged to go and meet Petula Clark, who was starring in *Sunset Boulevard*, in the West End. I had also hoped to clinch a double and home-in on the then *News At Ten* anchor man, Trevor McDonald, at ITN during the same trip.

With no news from ITN, well not the sort I was hoping for, I just planned for Petula. Then the day before my intended visit came the late news that Trevor could fit me in.

Trevor was delayed at the studios but managed to grab a colleague's office to undertake the interview. I even found out he'd toured the Isle of Wight playing cricket. Such a marvellous professional – and he can now go out in the evenings. He'll be delighted about that. After *News At Ten* he used to creep home to his darkened house, with everyone in bed, and suggested to me he was almost like a burglar creeping about.

After Trevor's interview, time was running short and I was some way from my 4 p.m. date with Petula Clark. I got lost on the way, too, and everyone I asked sent me in a different direction. When I finally found Covent Garden, I knew my running was nearly over. Thankfully I walked in as the big clock struck four.

I was intrigued with the 'phone boxes around London. They all seemed to be decorated with pictures of pretty girls, with not too many clothes on. I didn't have the time, money or inclination – besides, Petula was waiting.

A later trip to London unearthed a very funny incident. My destination was the Royal Westminster Hotel, Victoria, around the corner from the Victoria Palace. Bonnie Langford was due to meet us in the foyer. She breezed in, looking a picture of health, and the helpful management were going to find us a room for our interview.

Heather departed to enjoy a pot of tea and her latest Maeve Binchy novel. She left Bonnie and me to it. The friendly duty manager supplied a cosy room and refreshments. It was real splendour.

With barely six minutes on the recorder's clock, there was a knock on the door and the maid entered. We stopped the tape to find she was most concerned that the bed was not made up. Despite her obvious concerns we stressed there really was not a problem. After she left we both had a real giggle. Bonnie wondered just what she was expecting us to do in that hotel room. Obviously an interview was not on the maid's mind.

Later that night we saw Bonnie give a sensational performance in *Sweet Charity*. The Yank next to me said: "Who is this young gal, she's just brilliant."

It was a long way from *Just William*. I wish people would now accept her as a major British talent. Mark Wynter was also excellent in a cameo rôle in the show. Later I went back to the same theatre to meet Ken Morley, Reg Holdsworth from *Coronation Street*.

Another double came in early '99, when I journeyed up to interview Anita Harris and Jenny Agutter. Two lovely ladies, but quite different in character.

Just a week or two later I went for a treble – and just about made it. In a few hours I managed to chat to Fern Britton – with whom I'd once shared a chair at an Isle of Wight strongest man contest – at Olympia, David Mellor in his Saville Row office, and country music star Charlie Landsborugh in Guildford, on the way home. That was a hectic week with seven on-location interviews in four days.

With David Mellor in Saville Row. What, no suits?

In the summer of 1999, the Island's holiday industry had a major boost when London Weekend Television came to record *Reach For The Moon*. If only their press office had been as co-operative as the actors and crew. They were a joy to be with. The highlight was not me playing a window-cleaning extra in Yarmouth Square, it was interviewing three of the principal stars – Lynda Bellingham, Jonathan Kerrigan and Jason O'Mara.

Meeting many of my pop idols has also been a real joy for me. Walking into Adam Faith's dressing room and being given such a warm welcome was so invigorating. We could have talked for hours. I even managed to surprise him with a few facts. With both of us being *Archers* fans there was also a lot of serious business to discuss.

My lifetime affection for Ambridge was to finally end in early 1999. I thought the scripts were so predicable and trite, I just stopped there and then, after listening for well over thirty years. Interviewing Eddy Grundy, wonderfully played by Trevor Harrison, was a memorable moment, when their road show came to the Ryde Theatre.

How could it possibly be anything but pleasure when you come face-to-face with John Leyton, Bobby Vee, Brian Hyland, Eden Kane, Mary Wilson and the Supremes, Little Eva, Johnny Preston and Errol Brown? John Leyton, for example, had also been a Hollywood movie star and worked with Frank Sinatra and Steve McQueen, as well as being a friend of Elvis.

Eva – do you fancy a quick Loco-motion?

Andy Sharrocks, one of the best tour managers I've ever met, often comes up with top names. He lets you share back-stage life for several hours with the stars and road crew. It's such fun.

When Toyah Wilcox was booked for the Shanklin Theatre she agreed to come on my radio show, live at Sunday lunch-time. When I arrived at Dodnor there were people everywhere, most of them, including Toyah, playing street football outside the studio. The Bay City Rollers and the entire road crew had turned up. The prospect of Toyah and now, unexpectedly, the Rollers, on the same show set my pulse racing. That very night Richard Digance was also at Sandown – and he turned up as well. Nice party atmosphere to that radio show.

For one of my last (that's a real clue) interview stories, I initially have to go back to February 28, 1973, and a concert at the Winter Gardens, Bournemouth. Heather and I took Wootton shop-owners John and Myra Sweet, to a James Last concert. It was one of his first major British tours. We arrived in good time and headed for the stage door. I had several of his first vinyl albums with me, hoping to get them signed. Almost – but not quite. Fantastic show, though. The audience response was unbelievable.

We had parked in a multi-storey car park and went for a meal after the show, before heading back for the 3 a.m. car ferry. We had plenty of time – or so we thought. Then I wondered what time the car park closed. Whilst the meal was cooking I nipped out – to find it all locked up. That was handy. I went back to the restaurant with the news and we decided to worry about it after the meal. When the time came we saw no hope of getting the car out but suddenly had a slice of luck. There were alterations being made to the car park and there appeared to be a workmen's entrance that seemed very narrow. I was game to try and squeeze my Escort in between the gap. The side of the car actually gently rubbed against the wood but we put a rug in between and no scratches were visible as we inched our way out. I don't think we ever paid for that parking.

When later I saw that James Last was due at the Mayflower, Southampton, on Easter Monday, 1999, I decided to try for an interview. I had nothing to lose and there was only one way to find out. James is big business. Eighty million albums sold and over 200 gold and platinum discs. He sells out tours all over the world.

Back came a fax from Liz Pretty, in America, with the hint that it might be possible. There was a second fax, a week or two later, to say she was hopeful, but would not tell him until the day of the concert. I did a lot of preparation on the morning of the show but was never really confident that I was going to get a chance of an interview. We left on the 4.30 Red Funnel ferry, not knowing if the interview was on or even if we had tickets. The show was a 2,500 sell out.

We arrived fifteen minutes early and virtually went straight in to meet Liz Pretty. James could spare around fifteen minutes, despite having just undertaken two complete days of rehearsals and a sound check. It was the first night of his British tour. I went in and we hit it off straight way. Within a few minutes we were really having some fun. James and his lady were most hospitable. He took a look at the vinyl albums, many thirty years old, and signed the lot. He was impressed with the condition of the covers.

For one moment, during our pre-interview conversation, James thought he'd worked the Isle of Wight. Then he realised it was the Isle of Man. It wasn't until a few days later that I remembered a great story that was circulating on the Island in early 1978. Apparently the ambitious organiser of the prestigious BHC Ball, which was so popular at that time, with big-name bands like Ken Macintosh, had made an enquiry about booking James Last's fifty-piece orchestra. The agent had quoted £26,000 for the one night at Puckpool. I'm sure James would never even have got to hear about it. What would it cost today?

The actual interview took around seventeen minutes. James is not fluent with his English – but I can speak no German. It turned out fine, although once or twice I was not quite sure what he'd said. After a few minutes chat, James went off to the fifth floor for a meal. The tour, which included well over fifty people, had its own catering staff. "Come up and join us," suggested James.

We followed ten minutes later, after I'd packed up the gear, and when I had poured out two cups of tea, James signalled for us to join them. We sat down at his table and he wondered why we weren't eating. He immediately called over the chef and we had some wonderful fresh salmon and the full works. That was an unexpected pleasure. We even met his personal doctor. Outside there were at least four huge lorries and another four coaches, to transport the show around.

That was not all. We were given two £25 tickets in the stalls and sat with his lady and the doc. I wondered if it had all been a dream. Then I remembered Southampton had lost a vital relegation game at Coventry. Given the choice, I know where I'd sooner have been – and it wasn't Highfield Road. This was one of our most enjoyable Easter Mondays of all time. *Danke schön* to Hans Last (his name was changed to make it more commercial). He's now a multi-millionaire – and such a great guy. The plan worked.

CHAPTER EIGHTEEN

HOLLYWOOD FINALE

W HAT HAVE Charlton Heston and Sir John Mills got in common – other than being world famous film stars who have each made over a hundred movies? Within just three unforgettable weeks in the summer of '99 I interviewed them both and still wonder if it was all just a dream. Luckily I have the tapes to prove otherwise. I'd been spellbound by their films for as long as I could remember.

When Hollywood legend Charlton Heston came to Freshwater Bay's Dimbola Lodge in 1994, it was all too hurried for real interviews. The news media had a few minutes for a quick cuts-and-quotes press conference but time restraints meant it was all over in less than five minutes. Later I waited in vain outside the Farringford Hotel.

In hindsight, it couldn't have worked out better. Lydia Clarke-Heston, Chuck's delightful wife, came back in 1998 for her own photographic exhibition and we really hit it off during a ten-minute interview. Meeting Lydia for the first time is like enjoying the company of a real old friend. That cramped interview in a top floor stuffy Dimbola office certainly helped obtain that hour-long in-person session with Charlton Heston in London's fashionable Athen-aeum Hotel, where a penthouse suite was £650 a day and a standard double room £260 a day. Northwood photographer David White was also behind my scoop in getting the longest radio interview ever with Chuck Heston.

Charlton Heston and his wife Lydia at Dimbola Lodge, Freshwater Bay. There was not time for a real interview. That came years later, in a plush Piccadilly hotel.

(*By kind permission of David White.*)

On a steamy London lunchtime in July, I walked into the Piccadilly-based hotel to be met by two attentive and well uniformed doormen. Within two minutes I was seated at Chuck and Lydia's table and being offered coffee and smoked salmon sandwiches. As I sat in this palatial hotel I can remember wondering just what I was doing there. It wasn't your average seaside hotel. Here was the invincible 'Ben Hur' sat with old JH. Thirty-two million watched the eleven-Oscar winner movie when it was first shown on American television.

The obliging hotel staff found us a discreet and private bar for the interview. In the lounge Charlton was the source of so much fascination for other diners, residents and visitors. I'd never want to be famous.

When Chuck – he insisted I called him that – left to find the boy's room, I asked Lydia how long could he spare. I'd planned optimistically for an hour but was a little too scared to ask for so long. I suggested fifty minutes. "That should be okay. We'll ask him when he comes back in," said Lydia. "Fifty minutes!" exclaimed a startled Chuck. "We'll see how it goes." He must have enjoyed it. We talked for an hour – and were still friends at the end.

It was a little daunting but 'Moses' put me at ease.

I wrote to Sir John Mills and two days before I was due to see Chuck Heston, his lovely PA lady, Lynne Willis, rang up to say she'd just read Sir John my letter and he would like to invite me up to his house in tranquil Denham Village, Buckinghamshire, home for so many top stars.

Sir John, as I was privileged to call him, was asleep when I arrived around 10.30 a.m. At 91, and partly blind, he also had a back problem. This meant early morning massage sessions and he'd relaxed and fallen asleep.

I made friends with his two gorgeous dogs, whilst enjoying a cup of coffee. I was also aware he had a luncheon appointment. Suddenly I heard that world-famous voice. "It's John I'm meeting, isn't it? I can't forget that name."

Then he walked into the room – looking just like John Mills, movie star.

Great superstars have that magnetism and genuine humility to put you at

At home in Denham with Sir John Mills. A County Press 'colleague' suggested, at 91, he looked younger than me.

ease straight away. Nothing was too much trouble for Sir John. He was even happy to run over my allotted time. "Don't worry, I'm enjoying it. When I've had enough, I'll let you know," warned Sir John. Thankfully, that never came. I had also remembered his lunch date. After our forty-five-minute chat, Sir John remarked it was one of the best interviews he'd ever had. I was just thrilled to be there and to be in such hospitable company.

Just where could I go from Charlton Heston and Sir John Mills? I have a few ideas and only time will tell.

Not such a happy event in 1999 was the death of Johnny Moore, that marvellous lead singer of the Drifters, who'd appeared on the Island so many times, to great acclaim. Johnny had first joined the American group back in late 1954 and had sung the lead on many of their worldwide record hits. Twice he left to go solo but returned to the group. He was simply the face and voice of the Drifters. John was a quiet and gentle person and charming to talk to. The last time we saw him was at the Ryde Theatre. He'd been ill for some time with a breathing complaint and, at times, could barely stand on stage. The Drifters will never be the same again and the last link with their real American past is over. We miss you Johnny – and so do thousands of others.

Another Hannam hat has been reviewing shows. This began with the *County Press* back in the '60s, and really took off later with the *Weekly Post*.

At that time honest reviews were an innovation for the Island. The *Post's* attitude did upset quite a few people. Gradually the wisdom of honest reviews (it's still only one person's view) became more readily accepted.

Make no mistake, there were rude 'phone calls and some savage letters. It meant being banned from certain shows, but if you don't review honestly, how can you live with your conscience?

Back in the '80s I went to watch Leslie Crowther, who was a friend, on the opening night of his Sandown summer season. There were parts of the show, including Leslie's act, that I wasn't happy with. When he did a ten-minute lavatorial humour routine I found it rather embarrassing. He was far too talented to do that kind of cheap material. On the way home to burn the midnight oil, I was spotted by Leslie. He was such a lovely guy and, for once, I probably held back.

Later, Keith Huyton, the deputy editor of the *Post*, called me into his office: "That was the worst review you've ever done for this newspaper. You didn't like the show but were afraid to really say so." How right he was. It was a lesson well learnt.

I did have a major disappointment when I went to review Mike Yarwood for *The Stage*. For a long time I had been a great admirer of his talents. When he came to Sandown it really was a poor and dated performance. Sadly, the newer breed of younger impressionists had knocked him for six. I took no pleasure from giving that honest review. There have been others but, overall, I've been lucky enough to have witnessed some fantastic shows. I've always tried to write as a member of the general public – not a 'luvvie'.

In the year 2000, if all goes well, I'll celebrate ten years of *John Hannam Meets*, the longest-running show on Isle of Wight Radio.

I must admit to having been disappointed, in late 1998, when the show was moved from Sunday lunch-time to six o'clock in the evening. That was not my decision, but I guess I wasn't trendy enough for a lunch-time spot on their newly acquired FM frequency. For some time afterwards I was almost driven mad by people complaining to me because the show had been moved. I was almost frightened to go out. When I went to the Ryde Theatre, shortly after the change, I had about ten complaints in the first half-hour I was there. There was not a week that went by without several complaints. We still had a loyal following on Sunday evenings, but public demand eventually took it back to Sunday lunchtime.

I would like to publicly thank Andy Shier for his confidence in my show and to so many listeners for their support. In fact I would like to thank everyone who has made the show a success.

In 1998 I was delighted to be given the opportunity of my own television chat show on TV12, called *Hannam*. Paul Meade always had great faith in me and I hope I haven't let him down. I've still got so much to learn about the art of television. The best way to learn is in the hot seat. The crew have been encouraging and my studio assistant, Louise Gambling, a real treasure. Having the opportunity to showcase Islanders makes it really worth while.

Jimmy Tarbuck once told me you should always be nervous before any type of show. I certainly endorse that. Thankfully, people seem to like my work – or most of them.

With my late father having worked for the *County Press* for over fifty years, it was a very special moment when the editor, Brian Dennis, invited me to join them, in late 1998, as their *County Press* Awards organiser and judge. Also, writing features for the paper has been a great honour and privilege.

Perhaps the Bachelors did me a favour all

A TV12 studio welcome for two ex-Pan estate boys – Craig Douglas and Morris Barton.

those years ago by giving me a rough ride in that very first interview. That side of my life became so exhilarating. I was born a showbiz fan and have been lucky enough to pursue that dream.

My ambitions have never included wanting to perform on stage. I know my limitations. Compèring the occasional show or introducing the odd act is as far as I want to go. Even that has scared me on every occasion.

Basically, I feel I'm the man in the street who's been lucky enough to meet so many famous people. Some may be envious but it has been hard work. The support of Heather, Sean and Caroline has been so important. Mum and dad were a great inspiration and my sister, Celia, has also been a constant supporter.

I would like to take this opportunity to personally thank the hundreds of people who have helped me over the years. These include theatre staffs, agents, managers, press officers, tour and company managers, promoters, holiday centres, hotels, editors, photographers, fellow journalists, members of the public and, of course, the stars themselves. Without them I wouldn't have written this book.

So far, I've interviewed close on three thousand people and I still get that tingle of excitement every time I switch on a microphone or start to take notes.

Early on in my journalistic career I was often asked who I would most like to interview. There were five names that immediately came to mind – Cliff Richard, Sean Connery, Eartha Kitt, Pam Ayres and Richard Harris. That means only two to go. There were hundreds more on my hit list, many of whom you've read about in this book. My sights are now set on more super-stars of the same league as Charlton Heston and Sir John Mills.

There have been some regrets. My workload over the past thirty years has meant I've lost some close contact with friends. Socialising has been difficult. Watching at least a hundred shows a year is time consuming but very rewarding.

As far as I know I've only lost the close friendship of one person in my years in the media. That is much regretted. I have tried to rectify that, without success. I'm still such a great optimist.

How did that blushing teenager ever write a book? It's a wonder to me how I managed to even attempt some of my assignments.

Parky's confidence in me was perfectly timed. Many much closer to home have been equally important. Perhaps Maurice Leppard and Keith Newbery have a lot to answer for. Adrian Searle, who took over from Keith Newbery at the *Post*, has also given invaluable support. Thanks men. They and many others have worked miracles with my self-confidence

I've always believed my father, Roy, should have been a journalist. It was an unfulfilled dream. His encouragement and belief in me meant so much. That's why I've dedicated this book to his memory. With Sean following in the new Hannam tradition, he would have been very proud.

Taken by world-famous photographer Barry Lattegan, 1999.

OTHER BOOKS FROM
COACH HOUSE PUBLICATIONS LTD

COLOURFUL CHARACTERS OF THE
ISLE OF WIGHT

VILLAGE CHURCHES OF THE ISLE OF WIGHT

TRAVELLERS' JOY
– living and walking on the Isle of Wight

"QUEEN MARY": EARLY YEARS

LONG LIVE THE "QUEEN MARY"

All by Ron Winter

ALUM BAY AND THE NEEDLES

SHIPWRECKS OF THE WIGHT

Both by John C. Medland

WINGS OVER THE ISLAND
The Aviation Heritage of the Isle of Wight

By David L. Williams

PASTORAL PILGRIMAGE
– walks on the Isle of Wight

Written and illustrated
by Victor Vivian

GHOSTLY ENCOUNTERS
as experienced by Isle of Wight psychic
Margo Williams

ISLAND TREASURY OF VERSE

ILLUSTRATED TREASURY OF VERSE

ILLUMINATED TREASURY OF VERSE
– original illustrated verse

All by Lynn New

EMPIRE FOOD SHIPS 1934-1948
A Link with the Southern Dominions

By Richard P. de Kerbrech

MOTOR YACHT BUILDING
History of Silver Motor Yachts
– reprint of 1920s book

By John Bain

KING OF THE GOLDEN RIVER
By John Ruskin
– facsimile reprint of 1899 book
with additional bio-bibliographical study
by James S. Dearden

GERMAN WITH A SMILE
Beginners' German for the post-16 age group
and adults

By Helga Lees

Obtainable from:
Coach House Publications Ltd, The Coach House
School Green Road, Freshwater, Isle of Wight, PO40 9BB
Telephone and Fax: (01983) 755655